Of Course, I Can Do That!
A memoir:

Negotiating success in
the volatile "80's

Dr. Mary E. Mitchell

For permission requests, write to the publisher at:

Dr. Mary E. Mitchell
Author email: revmary49@gmail.com

This is not work of fiction, although at times it may seem to be with the volatility of the business world that I worked in. The people are real, but sometimes it felt appropriate to use first names only. It wasn't always who, but their position in the corporation that impacted my work at the time.

ISBN: 978-1-967349-10-4

Cover Design by: Expert Book Publisher

Edited by: Expert Book Publisher

Printed in the United States of America

PRAISE FOR THIS BOOK

Jeff Souza, President, Tehama Environmental Solutions, Red Bluff, CA:

"Of course I can do that!" is a fascinating window into the extremely volatile Pacific Northwest wood, pulp and paper industry in the 1970s and 1980s. Mary Mitchell graces the reader with her memoir through regular letters she wrote to her mother, as she was thrust into the industry as one of the few initial women in management roles.

The icing on the cake is "The Plain Vanilla Approach to Negotiation" that Mary developed to teach others that worked for her how to negotiate, which is a must-read for anyone interested in learning the art of negotiation.

Bill Carlson, Principal of Carlson Small Power Consultants (CSPC), Redding, CA

One thing that always struck me was the special relationship Mary always seemed to have with Red Emmerson, President of Sierra Pacific Industries.
Whenever I would meet with him, he would always ask about her. And if I needed to negotiate something with him, he would always give me the impression he would rather be negotiating with her. I don't know if it was because she was a woman in an unusual place or respect for her abilities.

Response to Bill:

Oh, how interesting! About six months after I left Wheelabrator, where Bill had been manager most of those years, I saw Red's VP, Dan Tomascheski somewhere in town. I asked how Red was doing since he retired. Smiling, Dan told me (and I confirmed it with him recently) that every time my name came up, Red would say "That damn woman never left a dime on the table!" What greater compliment could I ask for. Then Dan added that SPI management always thought highly of me. This showed me that the booklet I wrote on my top ten tips for successful negotiations works beautifully. Thanks, Bill, for triggering my memory of this!

Tad Mason, CEO, TSS Consultants, Sacramento, CA

Mary Mitchell's memoir brought up fond memories of an unforgettable time.

Nadine Bailey, Chief Operations Officer, Family Water Alliance, Inc., Colusa, CA

If you have anything to do with forests, trees and wood in the last 30 years, <u>do not miss this book</u>.

Or if you want to increase your knowledge about how decisions are made regarding western federal lands, <u>this book is for you</u>.

Or if you just want a great read about how a strong woman made her way to the top among some of the good old boys, <u>this is it</u>.

Reverend Sue MillerBorn, Senior Minister, Center for Spiritual Living, Redding CA.

It's been my privilege to have served in ministry with Reverend Dr. Mary Mitchell for many years at the Center for Spiritual Living in Redding CA. It was my honor to officiate the wedding of her and Paul and can attest to their devotion and love for each other.

I also know that Mary brought to the Center her lifelong managerial and administrative experience into ministry and helped guide and support the Center though changes over the years with professionalism and attention to the details of all aspects of the Center. It was my honor to serve with her as co-senior minister during transitions.

TABLE OF CONTENTS

Getting Settled in a World Marketplace
    Landing a job with a major corporation. Moving from
    lumber sales to buying wood fiber. What's a chip?
    Learning the import/export market and ways of corporate
    life. Why is it called hog fuel? Moving fiber by barges,
    trucks, trains and reloads. Why isn't my husband getting a
    job? Economic indicators and market assumptions around
    the world. The difference between pulp and paper mills,
    and intricacies of sawmills. Learning to love Oregon. Strike
    duty on a roll-wrapping machine.

An Office in the Basement
    Market studies: what's moving the market? Move fast,
    we're headed to the Olympic Peninsula. Working for two
    pulp mills and both managers dislike me. Finally getting an
    office...in the basement. When will my husband get a job?
    All hell breaks loose so good luck! Turning over stones and
    searching for fiber in Puget Sound and British Columbia.

The Mountain Blew and the Market Exploded
    Learning logger lingo. Mt. St. Helens begins to crack open.
    Flying our plane around the mountain the day it blew.
    Visiting a Canadian logging camp by seaplane. Getting
    involved in national forest planning. Watching an out-of-
    control slash burn. Finally, I get some help.

Crisis Reorganization Again, Again, and Again
> Another company reorganization. A new boss not pleased
> with a woman in his department. Unexpected subterfuge at
> the big meeting. Now a tugboat strike creates
> havoc. A house-husband really is nice. Oh, no, now the
> sawmills go on strike. Finally, more help arrives. Cruising
> the Canadian islands for fun, not fiber. What now…the
> pulp mills curtail. Another new boss and he likes me. A
> divine cruise on the Thea Foss. A kitten drains the stress.

Achieving My Potential: Chipping Doghair?
> The world's largest chipper is unveiled. The yacht club as a
> diversion. The lumber market tanks and now our mill is for
> sale. PIAs and KRPs then PRIDE. Confidence booster:
> Achieving Your Potential. Not enough stress…begin a
> master's program. The Sequim Bay plane crash. Marketing
> mix up for free kitty litter. No chips, so let's try chipping
> doghair. Crepes and beer in the woods – just like camping!
> The new 4000 hp tugboat.

Move: Yes! Move: No! Then the Sellout.
> Commodore 20, our first computer. Lumber market soars
> producing too many chips. An easy spring, then run for
> cover. Port Townsend is sold to Germans. Move? Stay?
> What to do? Go cruising. San Francisco calling, but so is
> Juan. Of course, I could work for him, couldn't I?

Reducing Stress through Stress as a Diversion
> No, twelve-hour days aren't stressful. Some peace and quiet on the ferry. Trying to sell the tree farm. Chips, sawdust, trucks, barges, then that darned train. The reality of processing doghair. Stress release in the San Juan Islands. Another pulp mill strike, so cut off the chips. Changing management for better control, then trying to control Canadians.

Goodbye "Diamond Z," Hello "Mary S." The three Mary's and one's a damned pushy broad. The happy face award. Time to push back. You really don't know why people are leaving??? Finally, a book about my life, "Stress and the American Woman." Renaming the Diamond Z. The big guns vie for Champion's mill. Dedication of the John Wayne Marina. Christening the tug Mary S.

The Terrible Stench of Fresh Cut Wood.
> It's only a chip reload for goodness sakes! Only two years and I think I understand my boss. Too many Doctor Nelsons. Paralysis from a Canadian tug strike. My husband romances my girlfriend. Looking for opportunities elsewhere. A marriage that can't go on. Would an Ohio girl really move to California?

California Calling and a New Chaotic Market
> From pulp mills to wood-fired power plants. Fiber is fiber, but what a unique market. One hundred semi truckloads a day seven days a week? The elixir called sunshine. Starting up ahead of schedule. Are you really Doghair Mary?

EPILOGUE

APPENDIX

DEDICATION

My heart-most dedication is to my Mother, Mary McIver, for her wisdom and guiding love, who raised my brother, Mike, and I in the most positive atmosphere anyone could have imagined.

For over forty years, Mother was the branch secretary in the Materials Laboratory at Wright Patterson Air Force Base in Dayton, Ohio after Dad passed away. Her boss was a NATO delegate, so her office was frequently busy with visitors from all over the world. As they waited to see her boss, she felt it was important to entertain them. As you can see, her office walls held pictures from the northwest and various mementos she bought when she came to visit.

I didn't know until after she retired that she kept my letters in binders <u>at work</u> and shared them with co-workers and visitors. She said co-workers would often take the binders home to read over the

Photo 1979

weekend. That made me blush! When she was in her last stage of cancer, Mother asked if I wanted the letters and, totally shocked that she kept every one, of course I did! After she passed, one of her bosses wrote me the nicest letter and said they all used to call me "Mary Jr." and everyone would take time to stop by her office and ask what Jr. was up to. She was always positive and engaging and a great role model.

1

FOREWARD

Jim Nelson, President of Nelson Facilitation LLC, Redding, CA

Mary Mitchell's memoir is a rich compilation of her travels through the highly competitive corporate environment of the pulp, paper, and timber industries in the Pacific Northwest. As a young woman hired fresh out of college, Mary got the toughest training available for complex problem solving. Her "Plain Vanilla Approach to Negotiation" reflects practical guidance for creating personal and professional successes.

Her work with the Western Shasta Resource Conservation District (RCD) brought enthusiastic structure to the RCD resulting in extraordinary grants, conservation projects, and support of the resources in her district. Her leadership attracted a skilled and committed team of workers to support the diverse array of projects they encountered. Whether engaging in stream restoration or wildfire fuel reduction, the RCD under Mary's leadership provided essential service to the community.

Mary's enthusiastic commitment, tenacious work effort, and intuitive insight has brought success and guidance whether to the timber industry, resource conservation and restoration, or to ministry serving the Centers for Spiritual Living. Her memoir is a journey through time demonstrating Mary's ability to identify and pursue the highest actions to be taken in diverse settings. She has brought forth great success while demonstrating love and compassion for her world and the people she encounters.

> *Every problem has in it the seeds of its own solution.*
> *If you don't have any problems, you don't get any seeds.*

Norman Vincent Peale

INTRODUCTION

The following letters to Mother were written between 1978 and 1987. The following transcript is almost word for word. I noticed I did use a lot of exclamation points, since the work was so new to me there were a lot of "WOW" moments to share. I left most generalities out of the manuscript, such as asking about family and friends, and things that would probably be boring to the reader.

The early letters were handwritten and then I purchased a typewriter and typed on 'onion skin,' which was the appropriate typing paper of the day. We finally bought our first computer in 1983, which made writing letters easier.

While transcribing the letters, when I had additional information that the reader might find of interest, I added "Note:" It was challenging to decide what to keep in, such as our expanding duck population when we lived in Sequim, or the diary of our flight around Mt. St. Helens the day it blew.

The 1980's was a very unique time to be a woman in a large corporation in the volatile world of wood products, timber, and pulp and paper. And in today's jargon, it was truly a man's world, and the dialogue I shared with her in the letters was so matter-of-fact, no exaggeration was needed. Looking back, I guess I really did break a glass ceiling or two. May these letters be inspiring to you or at least a bit entertaining!

WHAT I DIDN'T KNOW

When I accepted the Wood Fiber Supply Analyst job in Portland, what I didn't know was that the Pacific Northwest was in the middle of a boom-or-bust cycle. My job would be studying and analyzing a marketplace that was getting extremely volatile. Interest rates reached their highest point in modern history in 1981 when the average rate was 16.63% and it didn't decline to under 10% until 1991.

In his 1996 revised edition of "The Pacific Northwest: An Interpretive History," Carlos Schwantes, explained it all. In brief, as late as 1964, 30% of the lumber used on the East Coast came from the Pacific Northwest, but the revival of southern pine forests decreased the need for West Coast lumber. There was growing competition from Canadian lumber imports. Then, Japan shifted from buying lumber to only buying logs for their sawmills.

The northwest walked into a recession and, in some areas, a depression with more than a 25% unemployment rate. 60% of Oregon loggers lost their jobs. 48,000 lumber jobs disappeared!

1978

6/25/78

Greetings! On Tuesday I arrived and settled into the house we rented in Lake Oswego, Oregon. Reinhard and friend, Eric, had an uneventful flight cross country in our Cherokee 140 and it is now tied up at a small nearby airport. Eric just loved the flight and was sorry to see the end. He flew back to Ohio today on a commercial flight.

I was scheduled to start work a week later on Wednesday, but my boss, Rick Breuner, Manager of the Wood Fiber Supply Department, asked me to come in two days early to go through the desk I was assigned. The guy who quit had large piles of papers lying around, so he wanted me to try to put it all in some order. As I started rooting through the piles, a couple of chip buyers from the Oregon pulp and paper mills came in and invited me to lunch. From what I've observed, they are all very glad to have a woman on board and they are all anxious to teach me the business.

The next step up in this department, Wood Fiber Supply, is to become a chip buyer, which means negotiating contracts with sawmills to buy their wood waste for the pulp and paper mills. The wood fiber is separated into three products: wood chips, sawdust, and bark called hog fuel since it is smashed up by a hammer hog.

Rick introduced me to the people in headquarters and explained the orientation program. It seems there are two new Planner/Analyst positions that will go through orientation (I am one) with three other new hires. At the end of the program in October, we will have different jobs. One will work in the planning and modeling area. My area of focus will be wood fiber supply, which includes monitoring inventories, imports, exports, and usage. Wood chips and sawdust are used for making pulp and paper and hog fuel is used for fuel in boilers to create energy. It's a very, very complex job.

Right now, the unions at various pulp mills are voting on a new contract, and there is a chance they may go on strike. This means the chip buyers would try to refuse chip shipments from the sawmills, but they are under contract to accept them regardless. Once the inventory at a pulp mill is full, they have to store the wood wastes somewhere, but the question is where? I listened intently as they discussed the many options regarding locations, storage, transportation, unloading, and eventually reloading the wood waste after the strike.

On Friday, I spent a lot of time trying to get a handle on exporting. Crown Zellerbach's sawmills chip up their small logs and slabs to serve the needs of the pulp mills. All of the extra chip volume is sold to Japan. The buyers also buy chips from other sawmills in California, Washington, Oregon, Idaho, Montana, and Canada.

In order to determine what the chip price should be, they are constantly trying to find out what wood waste products their competition is buying and selling, the size of chip inventory at pulp mills in the region, anticipated changes in the lumber and pulp market, chip stockpiles at reload facilities, and exchange rates. That's why it's important to monitor what ships come into various ports to load wood chips and logs for export, the tonnage on board, and so on.

Wood fiber is moved from sawmills to the pulp mills by truck, rail, and barge. My boss is scheduling a tugboat ride so I can see how it actually works and understand the problems that arise in barge traffic on the Columbia and Willamette Rivers. It's interesting that Crown's two Oregon paper mills on the Columbia River (Camus and Wauna) get most of their chips by barge because the sawmills are far away and tend to be along a river.

Railcars are also loaded at sawmills, but to get the railcars to the pulp mill, at some point they must be switched from one railroad line to another, which is expensive. It's cheaper for the company to take delivery of the chips at the end of the first railroad line and empty the railcar onto property they call a 'reload.' The railcars are literally dumped or rolled over, and that's impressive! When it's time to reload the chips, vacuum machines blow the chips onto barges, which are then towed to the pulp mill. Crown owns its own barges and trucks. Enough about work, but as you can tell, it is very interesting.

When we went grocery shopping, we were surprised at the checkout—it is a new computer system that reads a box of squares with lines printed on each item. It took a very short time to check out. The computer reads the lines in all directions. The cashier quickly passes each item over the window and prints it out. Really neat! Another unique thing about Oregon is that they don't sell beer or wine on Sundays.

We looked at three different apartment complexes today. They were all-electric and the year-round electric cost, on average, is $8-15 a month. Energy is cheap, and the moderate temperature keeps heating and air conditioning costs down.

In July, my orientation program includes visiting the pulp mill locations at Camas, Wauna, and West Linn, and facilities at Oswego, WTCo and Lebanon. I will visit the Fairhaven pulp mill in northern California and the Cal Pac and Simpson sawmills. In Puget Sound I will visit the Port Angeles and Port Townsend pulp mills, and the Crown Zellerbach Tree Farm. My instructions are to observe and note chip usage, log facilities, species usage, species limitations, unloading facilities and limitations, storage capacity, testing and quality control, processes, and finished products.

In August, orientation included briefings on the 1978 third-quarter plan review, key economic indicators, chip buyer responsibilities, market assumptions, log requirements, fiber requirements, the inventory plan, and a 4th quarter plan presentation.

In September, I will go on customer visits to tour export facilities, import facilities, the managed forests, and logging operations. After that, my assignments will include monitoring exports to Japan, imports from Canada, hog fuel usage at mills, chip quality control at sawmills and paper mills. Later I will also be assigned to analyze fiber supply resources in the region and how to optimize the usage of different species.

We have plenty of paper plates and plastic forks while we continue to wait for our furniture to arrive.

6/29/78

We are adjusting very well to the new schedule and surroundings. We found a 2-bedroom apartment to rent and will move in two weeks. Hope our furniture shows up by then.

Sally Hood, an Ohio State Masters graduate we knew in Ohio, is also working for Crown Z in research. She told us she is taking a job in Omak, Washington as a Quality Controller. That is the job Crown initially offered me a few months ago. She is really excited about the job and moves in a month.

If the weather is good, we will fly north to see our good friends, Ben and Diane, on Saturday. We met them in Ohio, and now they live in Renton, southeast of Seattle. It should take about 1 ½ hours flying vs. 3 ½ hours driving. We haven't seen them for months. Ben plans to take Reinhard to his secret fishing hole and hopes to catch some steelhead.

7/13/78

My first business trip was highly successful. We flew to Eureka, California where we met Mac Brown, the chip buyer for our pulp mill, Crown Simpson. Crown owns half and Simpson Timber owns half. The mill makes pulp and ships it all over the world.

This facility is called a kraft mill. To make pulp, chips are put in a digester with chemicals to separate the wood into individual fibers. This mush goes through an 8-stage bleaching system until it ends up white. Now it looks like thick soup and is spread on a fast-moving screen while suction and gravity pull the water out. Then, it passes through hot rollers that press and dry the fibers at the same time. Then it is cut into pieces about 3' square, stacked and wrapped. It's sold to paper mills all over the world, where they just add water to get it slushy again and then make whatever product they specialize in.

The next morning, we started with a tour of Schmidtbauer Lumber Company, a huge lumber mill. We walked through the plant while the mill supervisor explained it all. I felt right at home. The wood smelled so good! This is one of the most innovative mills in the area. They work two shifts, one works 3 ½ days (35 hours/week), and they get paid for 40 hours. The morale is the highest and absenteeism the lowest of any mill around. Paul Schmidtbauer is about 35 years old and a real genius I'm told. He has the equipment to manufacture all of the machines in the mill, the planners, headrigs, resaws, hammer hogs, etc. At the moment they are building a boiler to burn bark and sawdust for energy to run the mill.

Later we went through Simpson's plywood mill where they were peeling 36" diameter logs into thin layers in just minutes. Next, was Cal-Pac Manufacturing, a Crown Z company that remanufactures redwood. Virgin growth redwood must be air dried for one year before it is manufactured into a product. Cal Pac buys dry redwood boards then planes them for siding and high-quality lumber. Second-growth redwood is made into fencing. According to Mac, second growth doesn't have the durability and built-in preservatives of virgin growth. Then we drove to Redwood National Park and walked among the old giants, just beautiful. Then we took a plane back to Portland.

Saturday afternoon, Reinhard and I drove up the Columbia River, through Hood River Valley. Wow, it is so beautiful and there wasn't a cloud in the sky. We made what is called the loop: 80N east to Rt. 35 south and back to Portland on Rt. 26. It was just like the postcard. We even stopped at the Mt. Hood Winery for tasting. Then we stopped by the big ski area at Timberline Lodge and people were skiing. It's July! They have one chairlift that goes onto a glacier and they run ski schools all summer.

Monday morning, one of the trainees, Gary, and I took off for Port Townsend and Port Angeles on the Olympic Peninsula west of Seattle. Gary has been with the company for 11 years in the accounting department. It was such a hassle to fly to the peninsula, so we drove. It took four hours, but what a beautiful drive.

I can see why Gary didn't get a promotion before this. He thinks he knows everything and tells everything he knows about the company to anyone who will listen. It didn't take long before I realized I should never tell him anything I didn't want everyone else to know. It's not hard to travel with him. I just let him talk and talk. He has been on this job exactly one week and he's already predicting who will be doing what one year from now. Oh well, it's this team spirit that I have to learn since we all have a job to do.

At the Port Townsend pulp and paper mill, we met the chip buyer for both Port Townsend and Port Angeles, Hal Hansen. He gave us a tour of the mill, which is also a kraft mill, and described their challenges. This mill makes pulp, paper bag stock, and multi-wall bag stock. The paper is not bleached, so they can use a lower-grade of chip because the color is not as important. But the species are important with a mix of fir and cedar for strength.

On Tuesday morning, we met the Port Angeles mill superintendent and toured the mill, which makes newsprint stock and telephone directory stock. This is a refiner mill, where chips are rubbed between two huge discs until a chip is just a mass of individual fibers. It is the only West Coast mill with a machine that makes very thin paper, which requires fresh and bright chips with the strongest fibers. If they have to add too much bleach to get the paper white, it reduces its strength. This poses many limitations and challenges for the chip buyer.

Back in Portland, I spent the whole day reading my mail. Since our department covers such a wide area and each person is specialized, the main thing is to let each manager, chip buyer, and analyst know what the other is doing, so I get copies of everything. Also, our fiber supply prices and pulp prices tend to move with the major economic indicators, so many magazines come across my desk tagged with articles to read, such as Fortune, Business Week, and about 10 others. One analyst screens all of these publications and highlights what's important to us. I have a lot to learn, and just now I heard that our Wauna paper mill announced it's going on strike tomorrow. It's a tissue mill that makes toilet paper, paper towels, and napkins.

7/24/78

A record temperature was set in Portland on Saturday: 98 degrees. It was very hot, but not humid. To get away from the heat, we decided to go camping. Friends recommended a lake at Cougar, Washington near Mt. St. Helens. We packed up and drove there Saturday morning. Everything was great until we decided to eat and realized all we brought was hamburger meat, one skillet, and paper plates… no matches, spatula, knife or fork, buns, etc. No stove, lantern, and many other things. So, we spent the day at the site and came home that evening.

Our furniture still hasn't arrived, and I guess this is a record for the longest time to move someone across country. The floor was getting pretty hard, so we have been sleeping on lawn chairs. We keep saving furniture hunting for bad weather days, the rainy ones we hear so much about, but it has only rained one day so far. This weekend, we must get with it and shop around.

Last week I was in Camas, Washington all day getting a tour of this paper mill. It was built in 1883, and at one time, it was the second largest in the world, employing nearly 3,000 people. The paper mill has 15 paper machines instead of the one or two I've seen before. I was there all day and didn't see half of it. I also toured Crown Z's Research and Development Center, which is huge. They have a miniature paper mill in one building where they can conduct all sorts of experiments. The chip buyer showed me around and explained the many challenges he has that I should know about when I'm analyzing market forces.

On Wednesday I was given my first project, but it was due the very next day at noon! I think it was a test to see how well I understood the mass of details I've listened to in orientation trips.

Every bit of it was important, not just nice to hear about. You might have read that all of the paper mills out here may go on strike. We have one out already, Wauna, and the other seven are in another union and may go out a week from today.

We also have three local sawmills: Rainier, Columbia City, and Estacada. If the seven pulp mills go out, the sawmills will have huge volumes of sawdust, bark and chips to dispose of. Our department has the responsibility to find all possible alternatives for these materials. There was a long meeting about this problem on Wednesday. Everyone had suggestions, but no one knew the best economic solution. My boss asked me to work on that and we would all meet again the next day at noon. Thank goodness they all offered to answer any questions I had in compiling that information, since the 24-hour clock was already running. Thank goodness I have my own form of shorthand to record the mountain of information they shared.

Well, the alternatives involve different sites that we could lease. All the sawmills could truck their chips to a site in self-unloading trucks and dump them. When the strike is over, the fiber would be reloaded and transported to the pulp mills. It was my job to get the costs together for each reload site, using both trucks and barges and costs for both unloading and reloading and to come up with the best solution. Well, I did it and when I presented my information, they were surprised. I got compliments from all and a very good one from my boss. He said it looks like I have a real good handle on the whole picture. Amazing!

A new alternative came out in the meeting, and that was to dump excess fiber at the Rainier sawmill. They have a lot of unused land that could be graded, a bed of sawdust laid down, and all three sawmills could dump their chips there. I was asked to go there the next day, check it out, and come up with the costs. My boss even let me use his car. Rainier is across from Longview, Washington, about an hour away.

It was a successful day. I met the Rainier management team, who took me to lunch at a local country club where we figured out the details. This is the type of work I will be doing in this position, planning alternative strategies and analyzing costs for each one. I don't need a lot of statistics and math skills, since a lot of it involves common sense and organization, and over the years these things have been done before.

I'm enclosing an article from Forest Industries Magazine, "Dozers Provide Muscle for Chip Handling Jobs." When chips are delivered to a mill or reload, the species must be kept separate, because each has its own strengths and weaknesses. Raygo Wagner chip dozers are commonly used to build the piles and later move huge volumes of chips from stockpiles to the reclaim conveyors. They can push 140 cubic yards or carry 75 cubic yards of chips at a time. The dozer bucket is 9 ½ feet tall! Georgia Pacific's Toledo mill has a crawler tractor with the world's largest chip blade, 28' wide 10' high, and 11' deep, weighing 24,000 lbs. It works 24 hrs/day and moves 12,000 cubic yards of chips a day. Needless to say, I'm totally impressed.

8/3/78

Guess I have been slow to write lately, but things have been a bit hectic. We have looked at so much furniture it makes us sick. Every store has about the same thing, but the prices vary a lot. We bought a king-size bed and there is so much room we only use half of it.

We're going to Omak, in eastern Washington next week to visit my friend, Sally, who took a quality control job at the sawmill. It's the weekend of the Omak stampede, a very big rodeo and I'm really looking forward to that. Sally likes her job a lot, but Omak is such a small town that she is finding it hard to adjust. She had to buy a bed from the Sears catalog and they only deliver to town once a week!

I was given one week to complete my next project, and was again considered a success. Our mill in Eureka, California is having a problem buying enough hardwood chips for making paper. This is going to get worse in the coming years due to the decreasing supply of hardwood trees in the forests. My job was to analyze alternatives such as contracting with a local sawmill to run chips especially for them, running another shift at one of Crown's sawmills, or building a chipping plant to make the extra chips needed, or doing nothing. I evaluated each alternative and put it into a chart and spreadsheet that will go into the presentation my boss will make to VIPs in San Francisco the following week.

When that was done, my next project is expected to take five months. My boss recently finished a study on the California paper mills and he and our economist are presently working on a study of the two Crown mills in Puget Sound. The next part of their study is about Crown's mills in the Columbia River area with four paper mills and three sawmills. They are so busy, and the deadline is the end of December, so they suggested I do it. My boss apologized several times saying it was quite an imposition on anyone, let alone a new employee, but with the threatening strike situation, it is their only option. It's a complex study involving the overlap of supply areas and suppliers. It's quite a challenge, so I expect to have my name on the front page when it is done. Then if it comes out okay, I will ask for a raise (at least that's the advice books give to women in corporations).

Today I sat in a meeting for six hours about the fiber supply plan for all of Crown's West Coast facilities for the next quarter. Things move so fast in the marketplace that quarterly planning is essential. The main question is: Where will the supply of wood fiber coming from, the volume by species, types of transportation available, sawmill production, pulp and paper mill usage, etc. Since I've been here, I've have had less then ten lunch hours to myself. The rest are working lunches paid for by the company. Today my boss mentioned the overhead for our department is getting a little high. I wonder why!

8/14/78

Our trip to Omak fizzled out because of the weather. Sunday, we drove to the ocean since the weatherman said it would be sunny, but it was thick fog and 50 degrees. We got back to Portland and it was 103!

Last Thursday was more orientation. This time the focus was on visiting two sawmills and a pole yard in Scappoose, Oregon. The pole plant is fantastic. Poles are 100-120' long and super straight. Everybody went crazy over them. When they bring the poles in from the forest, they debark and grade them for the best quality then cut them to the most profitable length. They are sold to electric companies on the West Coast and shipped by barge, rail, and truck. After they are graded and cut to length, they are peeled smooth. They only peel off what is necessary to make it smooth. If they peel off too much, the size may change and they might have to drop it into a lower-priced category, so the guy at the controls is highly paid so he doesn't goof up.

Remember my project on where to dump all the sawmill chips if the paper mills go on strike? Well, Rainier was chosen as the site, and the strike is underway, so I got to see how things were going on this trip. A bed of sawdust two feet thick was spread out over two acres, and all three sawmills were bringing their chips and the inventory was building quickly. The bed of sawdust keeps dirt and rocks from combining with the chips so when the strike is over, they can reclaim as many chips as possible.

The Rainer sawmill only has to move the chips about 300 yards to the pile, but that turns out to be the highest-cost item. Usually, Rainier's chips are blown directly from the sawmill onto a barge. When the barge is full, it is pushed to the pulp mill by a tugboat and another barge is immediately put in its place so the mill doesn't skip a beat. Now, having to stockpile the chips, they cut the pipe carrying chips and kept a semi-truck and trailer under it. The truck then goes the 300 yards where a portable truck dump was installed so the vans could be unloaded. And when available, they also hired 'walking floor' vans that are self-dumping. The two trucks and drivers at the Rainier mill work 16 hours/day during the pulp mill strike.

Crown has just purchased a paper mill in South Glen Falls, NY, and my boss was offered a management position there, which he readily accepted. He is headed for the top in this company and seems to be moving along fast. He has only been in his present position for nine months.

8/21/78

Friday night we took off for Cougar, Washington and the Lewis River. We had an excellent camp site right by the river and fished a lot. It rained off and on, but the air temp was warm and we had rain gear. On Saturday, we drove into the mountains on logging roads, some gravel and some paved. We saw the most beautiful sites even though there were low clouds. So many tall trees, clear lakes, and streams. We fished a couple of streams and only caught 7-8" trout, which we threw back. One of the lakes was dammed up thanks to hard-working beavers.

This week two more days of orientation and next week three days. Things are going well and it looks like there will be weekly meetings from now on about my progress on the study.

8/31/78

Last Thursday and Friday, I was in Cathlamet, Washington for orientation. This is one of our managed forests. We were given a thorough briefing including a slide show on how they thin, fertilize, and cut trees. They also spent a lot of time telling us how they monitor the forest for fires, do fire prevention work, and fight fires when they occur. It is very complex and too detailed to describe in a letter, but I was very impressed. In the afternoon they took us up to the logging sites. They cut 3,000 acres a year. In this way, they have about the same volume available every year in perpetuity. It's called sustained yield forestry.

Note: We were given a helicopter tour of the tree farm, and it was a low overcast day. The pilot had to snake around mountains and valleys to stay within sight of the ground while the whole time he was smoking a cigarette. I was a nervous wreck by the time we landed, because when Reinhard took helicopter lessons, he always said that two hands on the controls were imperative. I talked to the pilot afterwards and asked how he could fly with one hand and his knees. He said he had flown thousands of hours in Vietnam, so flying here was a piece of cake.

The logging systems that Crown Z uses are called either a cat, grapple, or high lead. After the logs are cut, it depends on the terrain how they will get the logs to the landing where a knuckle boom loader puts the logs on a truck. If it's level ground, they use a cat to pull the logs to a landing site.

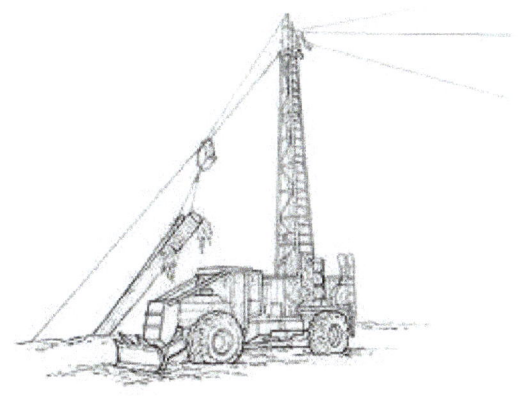

USDA Forest Service, Cable Logging Skyline Logging

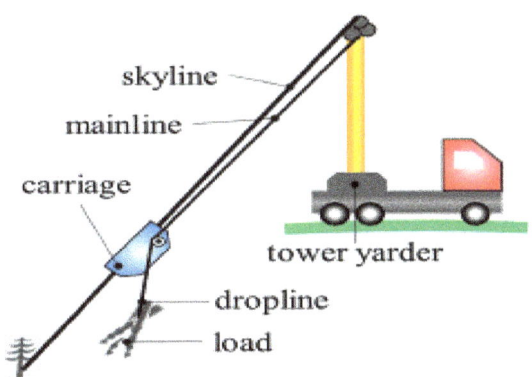

skyline

mainline

carriage

tower yarder

dropline

load

Grapple Logging Loading a log truck

If it's fairly steep, they use a grapple system where a tower and cable with a grapple are set up on the high end of the hill (the landing site), and a caterpillar tractor holds the other end of the cable at the bottom of the hill. The cable moves up and down the hill and after the grapple has been hooked onto a log, it pulls it to the landing site. The nice thing about this system is that the cat can move easily, so they can go all around an area without having to move the tower.

On Tuesday, I was in Estacada, Oregon. Our Timber Supply and Control Group purchases logs for sawmills in the area and most of the wood comes from the Forest Service. Timber Supply has its own logging crews and also contracts out jobs. We visited a very steep logging site, and I got to watch a skyline logging system. In this, the logs are pulled up to the tower and then cables suspend the logs as they are moved from tower to tower to the landing site.

Guys called choker setters wrap choker cables around the ends of logs on the ground, then the tower operator tightens the cable and the logs are suspended in air until they reach the landing site where, just as in the grapple system, a knuckle boom loader loads them onto trucks. As you can imagine, this is a slow process. When they want to get logs to the right or left of this location, they must move all of both the anchor and moving cables.

We went into the control room to watch the operator. It's a very noisy place. Often the operator cannot see the choker setters, so they use a horn system. When the chokers are coming back down the hill and reach the right spot, the choker setter sounds one toot. After they get the chokers hooked around the logs and are out of the way, two toots.

In case you are interested, the choker setters get starting pay of $7.20/hour and work a regular 5-day, 40-hour week. The guys felling the trees with chainsaws make $11-15/hour. They can make or break the company by felling wrong, cutting wrong, and either way, damaging or degrading the log's value. From what I have heard, Crown pays very well and treats their people very well, therefore turnover is minimal. They even paint the loaders, towers, etc., every couple of years to give the men more pride in operating a fine piece of equipment.

On Wednesday, we were back at Estacada to tour the old-growth sawmill, then on to see the Clackamas Managed Forest logging operations. We were so high up in the mountains we were in the clouds and couldn't see much. The logging roads were good, but just wide enough for the crew bus. Looking out my window I could only see space…it went straight down. Two and a half hours of that wore me out. Later, I found out other people on the trip felt like I did, totally exhausted.

In the high lead system, a tower is set up on one ridge and the other end of the cable is on the other side of the canyon, usually anchored on old stumps. The logs are airborne for a short distance and then are dragged up the hill. The dragging helps clear away debris and makes for a good site to plant the next crop of trees. They must plant the area within one year, since they want to get a new crop going as soon as possible. Planting season is not always the same as logging season, but they have it all worked out systematically. On the high lead system, they use chokers instead of grapples. The chokers are sent across the canyon, where the guys on the ground put them around the ends of three to four logs at a time Then they run out of the way as the cable tightens and the operator pulls the logs across the canyon. It has been a great experience to visit all of these operations.

A local paper gave an update on the strikes: Picketing continues at forty West Coast sawmills, plywood plants, and logging operations. The number of plants includes 13 owned by Crown, 19 Boise Cascade, 8 Georgia Pacific, 11 other companies, and 14,400 union members. There is no end in sight.

10/9/78

As you now know, Reinhard finally hooked a steelhead! It was so exciting! We met Ben at 7 a.m. at the Toutle River. We hit Ben's favorite holes all day and it wasn't until 5 p.m. that Reinhard finally had a hit, but what a hit: 10 pounds of fighting steelhead trout. Ben was right: green yarn and corkies. Less than an hour later he landed his second one, 8 ½ lbs. It was a great day!

Last Saturday I didn't have to work, so we went to Bonneville Dam to see the salmon. You have to be there to believe—so many fish travel all that way to die. On Sunday, we met Ben and Diane and fished one of the smaller rivers that emptied into the Toutle and it was filled with salmon. The fish were so thick it was sad and the river was so low that many of their fins were out of the water.

10/23/78

Our pulp and paper mills are all on strike and along with them are associated operations. Right now, I'm working at Flexible Packaging in north Portland during the strike. Gary told me I should volunteer for this duty, otherwise I would likely be sent to a paper mill working 12 hr. shifts. Flex Pack isn't too bad with eight-hour shifts, but last week I worked the graveyard shift from 11 p.m. to 7 a.m. The first couple of nights, I couldn't eat a thing, and my stomach was in turmoil from the weird hours, but by the end of the week, I was fine.

This week I'm working 7 a.m. to 3 p.m. at what is called a Dusenberry machine that cuts down huge rolls of copy paper into 50 lb rolls. I am at the end of the line and I stamp the end of each roll, wrap it with plastic, put it in a cardboard box, tape it and stack it on a pallet. When the pallet is full, I jump on the fork lift and take it to storage.

This isn't our plant, but it shows what a packaging plant floor looks like. Row after row of machines cutting down large rolls of paper into smaller rolls.

Last Sunday, we woke up early and it was such a beautiful day, we flew up to Seattle. Just after takeoff we could see Mt. Hood, Mt. Jefferson, Three Sisters, Mt. Adams, Mt. St. Helens, Mt. Rainier, and Mt. Baker all at once. Visibility was ~ 100 miles compared to Ohio's typical visibility of 10-15 miles.

Note: In order to keep the pulp and paper mills running during the strike, salaried personnel were assigned to each facility. At Flex Pack, if you were local, you worked various shifts Monday-Friday, but if you were from out of town, you worked three weeks on then had one week off. The company would pay out-of-town workers transportation to and from home during their off week or to whatever destination they chose, but the cost could not exceed the cost of a flight home. This became a nightmare for management. The people on my line come from the east, mid-west, and south. Many thought it was just one big party so on their week off, they went to Las Vegas or Hawaii and not necessarily alone. One mill manager told me his biggest headache during the strike was answering a call from a spouse asking why their husband or wife didn't come home.

In order to keep out of the wild and crazy "anything goes" atmosphere of strike duty, I started spending time reading books at my machine, because even the lunchroom became a pickup place. These people were determined to have fun, a lot of fun, and Crown paid for everything. One manager told me he turned down a request for reimbursement from one woman on my machine who had to buy a larger bra from this muscle workout. Amazing!

11/3/78

I have a break at work, so I thought I'd drop you a line. No end in sight for the strike. I'm doing the same work and probably will until the end. This week it is day shift. Next week I'll be on swing shift again.

It snowed in the mountains and yesterday it was so clear, Mt. St. Helens looked like a giant ice cream cone. I've been able to read books when the paper roller breaks down. I'm finishing a book a week, which doesn't say a lot for equipment maintenance here and the minimally trained operators.

I just got done with "A Rumor of War" by Phillip Caputo, a true story about his time in Vietnam and supposedly one of the best books ever written about Vietnam. I thought it was one of the best books I've ever read. Other books I've read lately are Paul Harvey's "The Rest of the Story," Shana Alexander's "Talking Woman," and Julie Eisenhower's "Special People." All are very good.

11/11/78

Tomorrow is my first Saturday off in a month and I'm looking forward to sleeping in. Next Saturday night, I'm the co-host for a party at work. I was one of three people who told the plant manager that a lot of the workers were getting depressed and needed a pick-me-up. The three of us were asked to put on a first-class party. The funny part is the plant manager said to tell everyone that the three of us were putting on the party and everyone had to pay $5. The manager didn't want other departments to have hard feelings, but really, Crown is paying for it.

It was the fastest $3,000 I ever spent! We're having it in the Red Lion ballroom with a disc jockey who plays disco and has flashing lights that go with the music. On top of that, there will be $1,100 worth of hors d'oeuvres and an open bar. Some people mentioned that $5 wasn't much to pay for all of that, and I told them that one of us had connections.

The mills and union are scheduled to talk again on Monday, but no one expects much. Boise Cascade made their final offer to the union with a 30% pay increase over three years and if the union doesn't accept it by November 15th, they are withdrawing the offer and bargaining will start again from scratch. If the union doesn't take it, they will be hanging themselves. I go back on day shift this week.

11/20/78

Did we ever have a storm last night! The wind was blowing up to 40 mph with snow. It started as rain, so this morning everything is covered with ice. I didn't go to work today because it required chains, which is a rare occurrence around here.

The party that the co-hosts and I organized was a tremendous success. The ballroom at the hotel was huge and everything was arranged when we arrived just in time to rehearse our parts for the program. A stage was set up with microphones, the disc jockey was setting up and there was plenty of great food. The two of us wrote a script for a program that was hilarious. Afterwards people couldn't believe we put it all together. At least it will keep everyone in good spirits until Christmas.

One day after work, I stopped by my old job site for a while. It was nice everyone still remembered me and they were glad to see I was in good spirits. They were very impressed with my muscles.

Last Friday, Mr. Carlson, VP of the Timber and Wood Products Division, came through Flex Pack to say hello and cheer all the department people on. I had never met him, but he knew who I was. We talked for about five minutes. It was nice of him to make the effort.

I'm enclosing an article about Mt. St. Helens. Scientists are saying it's 'near certainty' to erupt again, possibly near the end of this century. They propose more intensive monitoring of the volcano and preparation of a contingency plan to evacuate nearby areas. The last time it was active was between 1831 and 1856. They say one of the most serious dangers would be a heavy mudflow into the rivers. It would be a shame if that ever happened.

1979

1/12/79

We are experiencing the worst ice storm since the 1920s! Thousands of homes have been without electricity for three days now and will probably have to wait two more. Crews from Seattle and California have come to help with repairs. The problem is not the main cables, but individual house cables. The electric company has asked people to keep their porch lights on all the time so they can tell who has no electricity. I've never seen so many broken trees.

We hear this is the worst winter since the 1920s and it is still 100% warmer than back east.

This storm brought heavy snow to Mt. Hood. Today, Timberline reported 64" of new snow. We're planning to hit the slopes again this week since I will be on a swing shift. I like this shift because we can get to Timberline just as they open and ski for several hours before I have to go to work. It's so great to be on the slopes with hardly anyone else around.

Note: Workers at seven Crown Zellerbach Corp. paper mills in Oregon, Washington and California approved a new contract Tuesday night, improving chances for the settlement of the nation's longest pulp and paper strike. Of 3,828 workers voting, about 70% approved the new pact. Hooray!!!!!

2/5/79

One by one the paper mills have been settling, but Crown and Weyerhaeuser are the last ones. The union wants amnesty for the people who committed violence. Crown fired seven people because of it. One of them held a gun to a manager's head!

My new boss said he made travel plans for me in March, and is confident the strike will be over by then. I sure hope he's right. I'm finally off the 50 lb. roll wrapping job. I had trouble with my right shoulder, since it seemed to be separating, so now I'm driving a fork lift, sweeping floors, and tagging full pallets. It's pretty easy and very busy, so I don't have any more reading time, but the day goes by fast.

Ted's taking one load to the warehouse from our machine.

2/16/79

Well, things are back to normal after the strike. Last week I had a special project that had to be done in three days for a VP in San Francisco. My boss was out of town most of the week, so I had to handle it without his direction. I compiled information from six other people I interviewed, put it together, typed it up, and had it on the VP's desk the morning of the 3rd day. It was 11 pages long.

When my boss got back, we called the VP on his speaker phone and my boss asked about my report. He was very pleased and said it was "precise and accurate and probably the best report to come out of our department." I couldn't smile enough. My boss was so pleased, he sent copies to everyone in the department.

I also found out the job they were going to prepare me for is in Port Townsend, Washington, and is opening up on April 1st. Since the strike eliminated five months of my training in fiber supply, I don't think I'm ready for it. I see how complex it is and needs a strong confident person, so Friday I asked him about it. He was very glad to hear I still wanted to be a chip buyer, but he agreed I wasn't ready. He said I have a lot of potential, and he will work to get me into that field.

In this corporation, like all large corporations, it is not just how much a person knows and not how qualified you are, but who above is pulling for you. Now I know my boss is going to see to it that I go places. That is a load off my mind. I've heard from other people that my boss is highly regarded in San Francisco and has the confidence of the top people there, so I'm very lucky.

2/25/79

Oh, is it great to be back to work. I went in last Thursday and completed one short report and have a new one due Wednesday. So much to learn, but it's very exciting. It's an adjustment to wear suits again. Things have been physically moved around in the various departments. One person said during the strike many jobs got along just as well without people, so some of the 'deadwood' is being moved around. Some jobs are being phased out, but not in our department.

Here's a picture of Port Townsend. It is a community of two primary groups of people, hippies and mill workers. A lot of sailboaters, since the wind from the Strait is usually blowing for them.

3/26/79

Wanted to tell you that I received a flyer in the mail for a course on women in corporations and how to get ahead. I took it to work and showed it to the Employee Relations Director to see what he thought. I told him since I had never worked for a large corporation, it was taking me a while to learn the ropes. He read through it and said it looked like a great idea. He told my boss, and then signed me up and Crown is paying for it. Pretty nice! Of course, I have to give him a report, but I do think it will help me.

This week, the union workers at Flex Pack (where I was working) voted to go back to work without a contract. They think the union gave them the shaft and are trying to get their old union back, but they want to go back to work in the meantime. They could have done that three months ago.

What's the price of gas in Ohio? Regular here is $.689-$.699. Yesterday, we were happy to find one station at $.659.

4/8/79

Last Thursday a woman from the police department came to Crown to give a talk on rape prevention. The best preventive measure when out in public is to always walk with confidence and look like you know what you're doing and where you're going.

4/29/79

What a week! Didn't get a chance to finish this letter, so will try to do so now. This past Wednesday, I went to Port Townsend on the Olympic Peninsula on business and met with the management there and in Port Angeles. I also visited a Japanese sawmill and a timber company that only exports logs to Japan. I've been assigned to work on a study about the supply and demand for wood fiber in Puget Sound, so I learned a lot.

An upcoming problem is that the Canadian sawmills are expected to go on strike on the first of July and not go back to work until after Labor Day. Our mills get a lot of chips from Canada and our mill in Port Angeles gets 80% of their fiber from the Vancouver area, which has around twenty-five sawmills. My assignment is to draw up some contingency plans for getting other chips in order to keep our mills running during the strike. Logs will be piling up fast, so that will be my main focus.

5/15/79

Enclosed is a special treat, for me especially! My first big A-1 study is completed and you now have your own copy. It's a study on the supply and demand for hog fuel in the Columbia River area. Hog fuel is mostly bark and other waste wood that is processed in a hammer hog and burned as fuel, instead of using oil to make electricity. Two of our mills wanted to increase their hog fuel usage and asked me to find out where the wood was and how much they would have to pay for it.

No one has really monitored the hog fuel market because there has always been a surplus. In fact, until a couple years ago, we didn't have to pay anything for it except transportation costs. Now so many companies are putting in boilers to burn it, since the price of oil has gone up so fast, which means today, hog fuel is in short supply. My report was sent to seventeen people in the corporation who wanted this information. I presented the executive summary to my boss and his boss, and they were pleased. I am so glad I took that Technical Writing course at OSU!

Note: On May 18, I was offered the job as Chip Buyer for both the Port Townsend and Port Angeles mills. Although I technically wasn't ready for it, the chip buyer had been retired for three months and the looming Canadian strike was a major threat to the mills. It was a very quick decision by my boss and a very quick change for me.

The morning after I accepted the position, Reinhard and I drove to the Olympic Peninsula to find a place to live. That day we found a two-story house on Happy Valley Road in Sequim, rented it immediately, and drove back to Portland the next day. The following morning, I contacted the moving company and they said it was amazing that they had a half-full truck going to the peninsula that same day and they could be at our apartment <u>in an hour!</u> Oh, my gosh! No time to prepare! When the movers arrived, I was shaking so badly I had to sit down. Within 2 ½ hours, they packed everything, including the trash can with the trash still in it! We followed the moving van to Sequim. I've never had such a major lifestyle change take place so fast. I started my new job the next day.

You can see where Sequim is, in the red, .

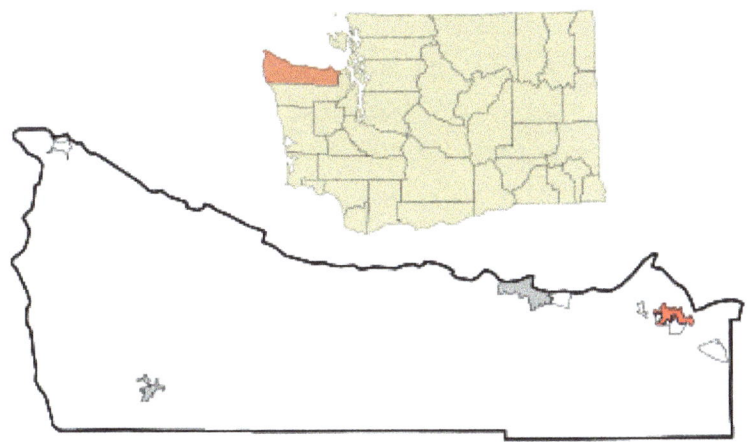

5/28/79

It will be a while before we get used to living here. It is so pretty and QUIET! It is a two-story, four-bedroom house on a country road. There is a pond on the property and a 2-car garage with a workshop. I've taken most of the curtains down so we can see the views since there are no other houses around us. We are about 1 mile up a fairly steep road and from the living room we can see Mt. Baker, which is north of Seattle. The only close neighbors are two foresters who live in a trailer on the other side of the trees well behind our house, so we feel like we are living in the wilderness. We took a ferry out of Port Angeles to Victoria, Canada for the day and, the next day back in Port Angeles, we drove up into the Olympic National Park just south of town. Absolutely gorgeous country!

My job is a real challenge since the man I replaced was here for at least 20 years. I sure have a lot to learn. My official job description says I'm responsible for assets of $1,477,000 and annual expenditures of $16,300,000. My boss was here all last week and we visited suppliers. My office is at the Pt. Townsend Mill and it takes me 35 minutes to get here.

My office is in the basement of the office building right next to the janitor. That says how much clout this position has with management. Actually, it works out really well since the janitor has been at the mill for years and he knows everything that went on and goes on…everything. He is a great source of information.

Since Hal, the previous chip buyer, has been retired for three months, it's taken awhile to go through the numerous file cabinets full of papers. He kept some paperwork for 20 years along with several duplicates of every page that were all neatly filed. When I found anything that looked like an agreement, I called the supplier and introduced myself. The janitor was a prince since most of the papers were so old it was disposal time and he was surprised how many trash cans I filled and kept bringing me more.

The challenging thing was to determine how the chips and hog fuel got to the mill. The man in charge of unloading barges and getting chips from the inventory into the mill had established himself as the key contact for the mill with the transportation companies and didn't want to give that up. He rudely told me to keep my nose out of it. I continued to hit a brick wall in establishing myself as the one responsible for fiber supply. One day I wrote down the name of the tug company, Foss Launch & Tug, found their telephone number and called. I asked to talk to the supervisor, who was Skip Brown. I told him I was new in this job and saw their barges tied up at the dock, and would he kindly explain where they came from.

Skip was initially speechless, but quite the gentleman and he offered to come by the next day and explain everything. I'll be forever grateful for people like Skip and Gary Deines at Puget Sound Freight Lines, a trucking company. I remember how shocked Gary was when he realized that I was basically dumped into my job. He took me to every one of the sawmills to show me how they loaded trucks for our mills as well as describing periodic problems in the system.

I had the same experience at the Port Angeles mill, but the person I was up against was the Mill Manager. He had the Controller as the key contact for suppliers and he liked it that way. It was fine with me at the time, since I had so much to learn. Every day, it was like drinking water from a fire hose!

6/3/79

We're having a lot of fun poking around Sequim (population 2,500). We found Butcher's Pole Yard where we can load up on free scraps of cedar lumber to use as firewood. We stopped at the grocery—there is actually one here in Sequim! The prices are lower than in Portland, which proves how high-priced Portland is.

At home we fed the fish worms and ants, pulled weeds, and enjoyed the scenery. We are surrounded on three sides by tall trees and with the ocean's cold temperature in the Strait of Juan de Fuca along the peninsula, it gets cool every evening.

It's taking time to get used to this small-town atmosphere. For instance, take dry cleaning. I took things in to be cleaned on Monday and asked if I could pick them up on Tuesday. No. How about Wednesday? No. Well then, Thursday. Thursday? Okay. So, I went in Thursday about noon and my clothes weren't ready. When I mentioned that she told me they would be ready Thursday, she irritatingly said, "But I didn't say what time!"

I spent this week in the office trying to get a handle on how things work. On Wednesday, my boss came from Portland and we took the ferry in Port Angeles to Vancouver Island. We rented a car and drove to Sooke about 30 miles west of Victoria to meet a potential supplier.

All of the suppliers I've met so far have accepted me very well. Everyone says it will take me about a year to get everything under control, but of course I am trying to shorten that by a lot. Tomorrow, I head for Portland for a two-day strategy meeting.

Our plane has been in Portland, so Reinhard is going to come with me and fly the plane back to Sequim where we will keep it at

Diamond Point airport, about twelve miles from home. While in Portland, I'll visit our Wauna pulp mill and go over chip quality with that buyer, Frank Misa, then on to Camas where that buyer, Rusty Hampton, is going to review chip quality and testing with me, then I'll head home.

Sooke isn't shown on this map, but it is on the first inlet north of Victoria on the west side of the island. You can see Port Angeles, where the ferry goes to Victoria. Beautiful cruise!

7/2/79

Most of the people I have to work with are very nice and helpful, but I am still having a lot of trouble with the guy who is in charge of unloading barges at Port Townsend. He wasn't going to give me an inch of room to do my job until I found the key, a box of cigars, and now he is just as nice as can be. He proudly went from office to office telling everyone I liked him so much I bought him cigars! Oh well, at least now we work together.

I am trying to spend my time equally divided between Port Angeles and Port Townsend and the mill managers are fine with that. I talk to the barge companies every day, both American and Canadian, plus to some suppliers to find out when barges will be loaded, what species they are cutting, and things like that since we have a certain species mix we have to have on hand at both mills. My boss in Portland and I talk a lot since I am still unsure about some things.

The Canadian sawmills and pulp mills are in the middle of negotiations and could go on strike next week. Our Port Angeles mill gets eighty percent of their chips from Canada so lately I've been stockpiling chips, which is very risky since if the chips lose too much brightness we'd have to burn them for fuel. If the Canadians don't go out on strike, I may have to hire an auctioneer and sell chips by the bag full!

The lumber market is in a downturn because of the slowdown in housing starts. I read recently that conventional thirty-year fixed rates for mortgage loans are 11.9%. If we lose any supply, then I'll learn a lot about how to find chips that I don't even know about! I'm told the market seldom reaches a state of normalcy around here, but that's what makes the job interesting.

Port Townsend recently lost its biggest chip supplier who will stop delivering to us January 1980, so I have six months to replace that supply. Now that is a challenge! There are a lot of sawmills in Puget Sound, but most are under contract with other pulp mills. I will be visiting as many of these sawmills as possible to find out what is available and maybe I can out-bid our competitors to take a supplier away. In a tight market, that's the name of the game.

7/19/79

Last week I was in Canada for a day. I flew up to Vancouver in the morning and back in the afternoon. One of the Crown Canada managers took me around to visit a Crown sawmill and two others that we buy chips from and a reload facility that unloads railcars of chips and reloads them onto barges.

Last weekend I had fire watch duty so we had to stay home. When the risk of fire on Crown's timberland on the peninsula is moderate to high, someone has weekend duty. If a fire does start, the State Dept. of Natural Resources will call me, then I have a list of thirty people to call to action. The fire danger ratings are Level 1-5. On a Level 3 day the State flies over the timberlands. On a Level 4 day, Crown hires someone to fly over the timberland as an extra precaution. On a Level 5 day, firefighting crews are on standby alert and pilots are in the air all day. Crown wants to sign Reinhard up to fly for them when needed. We are checking into the cost of insurance, etc. He would sure enjoy it and I would enjoy just the thought of him finally working.

7/28/79

So much has happened lately, I better get a letter off to you before I forget any of it. The biggest thing is that Reinhard did start flying for Crown on fire patrol. He flew 3 ½ hours this week already. The company that usually flies fire watch has had so much business they don't have enough planes and pilots available on short notice. When the day is a Level 4 or 5, he takes someone with him to be the spotter. My girlfriend is a college student and she has been available to be his spotter. She reads the maps as they fly, and when they see smoke, Reinhard reports it to the home base operator. On Monday he flew some of Crown's engineers around to look at logging roads.

There is a chance he can get an air taxi rating and fly people for hire. New regulations were issued this year by the FAA on air taxi. He can fly for hire only on VFR days (clear days using the Visual Flight Rules) if he has 500 hours flying time and abides by all other regulations. It is a real hassle to get the certificate, but he is checking into it. There are 300 regulations he has to follow to get this rating. A lot of people are encouraging him to do it, so we will see what happens.

Last week there was finally a dinner for Hal Hansen, the retired chip buyer I replaced. It was a prime rib dinner with about twenty-five people who said really nice things about Hal. I was the only female and was treated well and made new friends with some of the pulp mill management team. It's important because they are the ones who do the most complaining about chips—too many, too little, poor quality, etc.

Last Thursday, Foss Launch and Tug Company, which owns all of the chip barges and most of the tugs in Puget Sound, had a cruise along Hood Canal that included an open bar and buffet dinner. It was specifically for Crown people associated with chip handling. Husbands and wives were included, so Reinhard went along and it was just wonderful. It was a suit and tie affair and we boarded the Thea Foss at 6 pm. It was built in 1929 and owned by John Barrymore at one time, who cruised it around the world. It is 120' long and 21' wide. Foss bought it about 20 years ago just for entertainment purposes. The cruise lasted until 10 p.m. The scenery was breathtaking, the baby blue sky with the outline of the Olympic Mountains.

On Saturday we ran out of water at home. We get our water from the Dungeness River through a network of open ditches that also serve other homes in the area and apparently the flume plugged up. Until it's fixed, we won't receive water. We do have a thousand-gallon storage tank, but I don't know how long that will last. The water also stopped running into the pond. One neighbor stopped by and said the man in charge of the ditch system is 77 years old and is not as speedy as he used to be. The neighbor has 100 head of cattle so he is really concerned. We are rationing what water we have and hope we can take a shower Monday morning.

Reinhard thought that it might be a good idea to open up the water storage tank and see if it needed to be cleaned. He took off the cement top and jumped in. The water was just below his waist. All of a sudden, he jumped up and said something was swimming around his feet! I went for a net and he caught a fish about 5" long that was white, like an albino, and blind. Who knows how long that fish was in that tank, our drinking water tank!

On Sunday, I went out to the pond to feed the fish and not one swam up. I threw a handful of feed and the water was completely still. I threw more and nothing happened. I looked and looked and could not see one fish. I called the sheriff and, of course, nothing could be done. I figured someone came in and cleaned out the pond.

I asked the neighbor if she had seen anyone, but she didn't even know we had a pond. I just couldn't sleep all night thinking about those fish, especially old Moe, the largest one with one blind eye.

On Monday, I was depressed all day wondering who would do such a thing. That evening, I was mowing the grass by the pond and saw a fish. I threw a lot of food, but nothing. A half-hour later, there was a splash and then it seemed like 4 or 5 were eating. I felt like I was in the Twilight Zone. It was the strangest thing I ever experienced. The next morning we woke up and there was a blue heron by the pond. These herons stand 3' tall and are great fishermen. Now we know the fish were just hiding. They're all out in the open and back to their normal behavior. Old Moe is still there, but instead of sixteen fish, we only have eleven. The smallest one left has a big gouge in his back where the heron poked him. We learned a lesson about living in the country and strung wire in a crisscross pattern across the fence over the pond.

Driving to work the other day a huge black bear ran across the road in front of me. A bear! Yesterday I saw a woman walking her dog along that same stretch of road and I thought she must be crazy.

The Wood Fiber Supply Manager from Portland, Rick Breuner, was up here last Thursday for a meeting with the chip handling people at Port Townsend and mill management. I was also there with my immediate Portland boss, Don Hansen. The mill managers were quite accommodating, which was unusual. After the meeting Rick said he was very pleased with my progress and hoped I liked the job, but if I had any reservations about it, there was another job opening at Wauna and I could transfer there, no problem. I told him I really liked it and thought I could do a good job here and wanted to stay. He was glad, because he wanted me to stay also. It felt like I received a gold star and a pat on the back. It feels good that I have 100% backing from Portland.

10/3/79

The day after our Portland manager left, the Port Angeles mill manager wanted to meet and he abruptly told me that he was putting the plant controller in charge of the chip and hog fuel responsibilities. He felt it was imperative that he have control over it. That meant I would be pretty much in the dark about operations there, but he did show me a desk I could use if I had to, but that was about it. It didn't even come with a telephone. But, the next thing that happened is the controller went on vacation and the whole mill 'went to hell' so to speak.

I stopped by the mill on Tuesday and they were out of hog fuel and hemlock chips. The manager stridently asked if I could fix it. I said "Of course!" while hoping I could. His response was "Then fix it!" Together with the refiner mill superintendent (who uses the chips) and the utilities superintendent (who burns the hog fuel), we had the whole mill humming in two days.

On Friday, I put together a package of duties I was ready to assume at Port Angeles, got approval from my boss and it was a piece of cake to get the green light from the mill manager. When the controller came back from vacation the next Monday, he found out that he was the controller again, not a chip buyer. Such is life.

Delete this paragraph: I don't think I told you that Port Townsend is called a 'kraft' mill which uses chemicals to cook the chips until the individual fibers separate. Port Angeles doesn't use any chemicals since that would impact the brightness of the paper. Instead, they use refiners, which one pair has two huge stainless-steel plates with small ridges and when the chips are in between the plates that move at a high speed, it rubs the chips against the ridges until the fibers separate. The result is consistently high-quality wood fibers that can be made into high-quality, bright paper.

Paper brightness is measured on a scale of zero to 100 and it is the amount of light reflected from the surface of a white sheet of paper. At Port Angeles, their paper brightness must be at the 91 level, which is high, and that gives more contrast between the sheet and the text and images, resulting in bolder images. It's why they can make newsprint and also very thin paper for Bibles and other specialized uses.

For the past three weeks I was focused on organizing the flow of wood supply in my mind. The only background data I had to work with were the mill's monthly financial statements and the invoices I approved to pay for deliveries. Now I have it pretty well organized and have a good working relationship with the suppliers and our key contacts at Crown Canada Fibre Supply: Phil Musgrave, Mike Thompson, and Murray Hall.

The Port Angeles mill manager continues to be very difficult to work with, because he does not delegate any responsibility and surrounds himself with 'yes' men. I don't play that game, which may be a thorn in his side, but that is okay since my real boss is in Portland.

Next week, I go to a week-long seminar in Portland on problem solving. About two dozen people will be in the class, timed perfectly since it is ironically called "The Rational Manager."

10/16/79

The class was excellent. We worked in teams for <u>fourteen hours every day</u> just to problem-solve. I've already put it to work. We learned a systematic approach to choice analysis, cause analysis, risk analysis, and planning.

Then it was great to spend a really quiet weekend at home. We had the fireplace going the whole time. Last week we bought a Stihl chainsaw with a 20" bar, the brand most loggers use. We can cut wood on a Crown clearcut not too far away.

I had to return to Portland for an anti-trust meeting on Monday. I took the 6:30 a.m. flight out of Port Angeles and got back home by 5:30 p.m. The meeting was a presentation by a corporate lawyer about what we can and cannot say in the world of pulp and paper and wood products, what language is illegal, and how it could lead to a criminal conviction on price fixing. It almost makes me paranoid, since I work in a position where I talk to competitors a lot.

The corporate policy is that I have to hear this speech at least once a year and sign a statement saying I understand it. It requires that if I am ever in a situation, a meeting, in a restaurant or bar, where a competitor even mentions or insinuates prices, I must state out loud that our company policy does not permit me to be in this conversation and then leave.

Next week, I have to go to Portland on Tuesday and Wednesday for a forecast meeting. I don't mind the flight down and back since the Port Angeles flight goes to Seattle where I get on an Alaska Airlines flight to Portland. On the flight back, they always serve warm nuts and champagne. A nice way to end a busy trip.

11/19/79

This morning, I had to be in Everson, WA by 10 a.m. near the Canadian border to visit a sawmill that has a couple of rafts of cedar logs for sale. The owner and his plant manager took me out in their 34' Bayliner to see the logs. As we were by the rafts, the manager suggested we have a drink and poured each of us some bourbon and coke. We discussed quality, quantity, and price, and then he poured us another drink. When I recognized that they weren't interested in the logs, but more interested in me, I went back to quality, quantity, and price and said it was time for me to head home, since it was a long drive back to Sequim. That was fine, but they were disappointed and we never did come to an agreement. On the way home, I stopped at a 7/11 and bought a quart of milk and downed it so I could get home safe and sound.

Housing starts are really dropping and interest rates are rising, so a lot of sawmills are curtailing shifts or shutting down temporarily. The result is fewer chips are coming in and our inventory is dropping fast. I have been very busy looking for extra chips everywhere and I'm not having much luck. I'm going to look at an old stockpile of chips today that's a few miles inland. I might be successful if I can get the chips reloaded onto a truck and loaded onto a barge at the right price.

11/28/79

I had to pick up a potential supplier at the marina in Port Townsend this morning who asked for a tour of our mill. He wanted to see for himself that our chip handling system was well-maintained so that if we had a problem it would not impact his mill's output. He has a sawmill on the east side of Puget Sound about 50 miles north of Seattle. He cruised over in his 40' power boat and tied up at the marina. After the tour, we had lunch and it went well. Chances are good we will be buying his chips soon.

As chips get harder to find, tempers at the mill flare easily. I try to keep everyone level headed, but the problem is everyone is trying to cover their rear end instead of trying to cooperate and get the job done. One good thing is my office has been moved out of the basement to the first floor. I think it is so they can keep a close eye on me, but it is nice to at last be in a room with a window. I use a corner of the blackboard in my office to write the date I expect we will run out of chips (if I can't get more creative), just so everyone knows. The mill manager reminds me every day that if Port Townsend runs out of chips, my name is at the top of the list to get transferred to St. Francisville, Louisiana, where another Crown pulp mill is on strike. A lot of people are being sent there for good-old strike duty.

With the bad lumber market, the price of logs is very high. Our largest supplier of sawdust and hog fuel is shutting down for the whole month of December. Now, the free hog fuel I could have purchased three months ago has vanished. I located a large stockpile of cedar chips in Cosmopolis, WA on the coast and will go there Friday to bargain for them. We would have to bring the chips to Port Townsend by a large ocean-going barge. It is a real scramble to fill in the increasing shortages.

12/11/79

Enclosed is an article on how Christmas trees are processed in Christmas Town USA, Shelton, WA. Thought you might enjoy it. Shelton is home to Simpson Timber Company and their sawmills are my largest suppliers. The mill manager, Marv, is one of a kind. Like most of my suppliers, we have a three-year contract where either side can ask to renegotiate the price every quarter. On any one day, I'm either preparing to negotiate, negotiating, or writing amendments to our agreements. Right now, I have over four dozen or so contracts in place. Quarterly negotiations are common since the lumber and pulp and paper markets are changing so fast.

Marv is a perfectionist and only allows me fifteen minutes to present my case on what I think the unit price should be for chips, sawdust, and hog fuel for the next quarter. But with Marv's detailed attention to the marketplace, in order to satisfy my position on prices, it requires constant homework on my part and lots of traveling. For instance, I have to monitor how many shifts the sawmills in the region are running, finding vantage points so I can see the log inventories at sawmills, chip inventories at the pulp mills in Puget Sound and British Columbia by species. Then I check records at the ports to find out the volume of fiber coming into Puget Sound from Canada and the volume leaving Puget Sound for Japan; plus monitor various market indicators such as housing starts and interest rates.

Prior to a meeting with Marv, every quarter I gathered all of the information and would stop at McDonalds in Shelton an hour before my meeting to go through my checklist. It's a system I created to help me finalize my position on why the price should change up or down on the three products I purchased from him. For example:

- How have chip/sawdust/fuel inventories at pulp and paper mills in the region significantly gone up or down?

- Have both log and lumber inventories at sawmills changed up or down?

- Check reload facilities to see what changes there are in any stockpiled wood fiber.

- The volume of chips in inventory at port facilities waiting to be exported.

- The prices of chips that have been exported, which is printed in an export quarterly newsletter.

- The volume and prices of logs that have been exported this quarter, also available in their newsletter.

- Knowing of any strikes or walkouts going on that are impacting the wood fiber supply.

- Which sawmills have changed the number of shifts they run, which determines output?

- Identify any other fiber movements that impact the price in my region.

The result is a checklist or spreadsheet on these items and, as I told my boss, the conclusion as to whether prices on X, Y, and Z should go up, down, or stay the same "kinda falls out the bottom," which made him laugh.

At Simpson, Marv waits for me to present my case first so that he can try to poke holes in it and almost all of the time he can't. We easily came to an agreement within fifteen minutes.

I'll never forget one quarter when my checklist of the up-or-down market indicators showed considerable downside, so I felt that

I could decrease Simpson's prices by 30%. I shared it with my boss and he checked with the other chip buyers. They all said there was no way I could do it. I bet them each a fifth of Crown Royal whiskey, and low and behold, I ended up with five-fifths of Crown Royal!

I just found out that I have a new boss temporarily. He is one of our department managers, Jim Oswald. The Columbia River pulp mills are having just as many problems as I have, but they have enough chips to last until January. I was sure we would have to shut down by December 1st, but things change daily. It feels like I'm beachcombing, walking along the beach turning over every stone to find a treasure.

One example is we have enough sawdust to last three more weeks and I haven't been able to find any extra in Puget Sound or Canada. Just today, one of my arch competitors, ITT Rayonier in Port Angeles, came across a barge of sawdust and called me. Within an hour I purchased it and, of course, now I owe him a favor, which he loves.

Anyway, my new boss and I get along just wonderfully. He is a Stanford MBA graduate and top-notch. He has been visiting some of my suppliers without me and talked to co-workers in the pulp mills and told me he gets very good feedback about me, which I'm glad to hear.

This is a time of crisis when everyone is trying to cover their 'you know what,' so some people that I thought would be cooperative are not. The reason it's so good to have a new boss is that the others didn't have time to worry about Puget Sound since they have plenty of problems in the Portland area.

Port Angeles continues to run on less than a four-day inventory, which means daily drama. Dozens of sawmills are shutting down or cutting back 50%. Yesterday there was less than a one-day supply of hog fuel on the pile, so you can imagine how stressful that was.

Bright paper coming off the line at Port Angeles.

This week, a landowner west of Port Angeles called me to say he had a canyon filled with bark. I went there and he was right. For years there was no marketable use for bark from the sawmills, so he allowed people to dump it in his canyon. He covered it up with a layer of dirt, so the bark shouldn't be that wet. I'm working on locating equipment to dig it up and a portable grinder to process it, and get it to our mill. I find it fascinating when things happened years ago and I hear about it just in time.

12/18/79

Winter winds are here and for the last three days it's been up to 50 mph on the strait. That means barge traffic is slow, and barges from Canada can be up to a week late. We had to start up the old woodmill and chipping plant at Port Townsend, which can chip logs up to 30" in diameter. Just looking down the chute at how fast that tree gets chipped is scary. The woodmill hasn't operated for five years, and it feels like you're walking through an ancient museum.

I worked up a plan for how many logs I needed and tried to turn it over to the Timber Department (of which we are a part of now). They only deal with logs… every day...but they weren't interested. I had to appeal to the managers in Portland for help. It was a major hassle, but they finally relented. There is always this underlying competition between timber and pulp and paper. Who knows why? Perhaps it's like two children whose parents (headquarters) treat them differently at times. It seems like the chip crunch will be with us for at least six months, and chips will command a premium price for the whole year. It's going to be difficult to say welcome to 1980, but here we go!

1980

1/6/80

The pulp mills are still running, since every week I find extra chips or sawdust to keep us going. Some of my suppliers are saying the squeeze is just beginning. My new boss is campaigning to get me the full-time assistant I need, thank goodness. I totally look forward to that. He also gave me some good news. It seems there are very few women in Crown that are interested in transferring or being promoted.

The head of personnel, Bob Davis, recommends people for promotion. He took my boss to lunch to find out how I was doing. Jim explained it all and Davis is going to help me get an assistant. Jim says if I can hang in there for another year and prove I can be a pro – project a professional image- I will be up for another promotion. I was glad to hear that, but I imagine someday I might decide I've had enough of this. There is so much game-playing and back stabbing in the corporate world. If you can't cope with it, you won't make it. I just accept it for what it is—power plays. Anyway, things are still going well, although it's challenge after challenge, which keeps me alert and busy.

1/23/80

Work has been going pretty well. Last week our department was taken away from the Wood Products Division and given to the Timber Department, which means we will have a different VP. Our department head will likely get replaced. This will also mean the log managers and chip managers will be forced to work a lot closer. Hallelujah!

1/28/80

Strange as it may seem, it is really cold here. It got down to 17 degrees last night. Most of the sawmills had to shut down, and at Port Townsend the yard equipment wouldn't work, so trucks couldn't be unloaded. At Port Angeles, the chip belt that moves chips into the mill was frozen and we were within two hours of shutting the whole plant down when they got it fixed. No one is prepared for this kind of cold here.

/10/80

On the way back from Seattle today, we took the pontoon barge/ferry across the Hood Canal. We were in the middle of the canal when the barge stopped. There was a lot of activity around the tugboat, which was tied to the barge for power. It was cute…all the men got out of their vehicles to see what was going on, including Reinhard. They were all lined up against the railing watching. Wished I had a camera. Apparently one of the ropes broke that had held the tug to the barge. The men were satisfied when they watched a new line being secured to the tug and away we went.

2/18/80

I had an interesting thing happen last week. I was visiting one of my chip suppliers to sign a contract amendment. It is a small supplier, but in this market every supplier is important. The owner, Vern, told me that he was flying back from Palm Springs the previous weekend and sat next to Denny Denman and asked if I knew him. Denny is one of our Executive VPs who reports to the president. Anyway, they talked for over and hour and Vern told him what a good chip buyer I was and how hard I worked. I can imagine or maybe I don't want to imagine what he said. As he was telling me this, he said they also talked about women's lib, and I almost gasped!

Well, the next day, I got a call from one of the men I worked with during the strike, who was in corporate communications in San Francisco. He said he was in the president's office reviewing a project he couldn't tell me about. He had me in mind for it when in came Denny and another VP. The president asked their opinion on the project and Denny said he thought Mary Schroeder would be perfect for it. My friend said his mouth dropped open, and he told them he was thinking the same thing! Denny related the story of meeting Vern on the plane and emphasized that I was not just concerned with the quantity of chips, but also the quality. Then my friend relayed how we worked in the 'war' (at Flex Pack) and put that great party together. Needless to say, I was shocked yet very pleased. I haven't heard what the project is and usually the way it works is all details would be worked out before I would find out I was even being considered for it. If nothing ever comes of it, at least I don't have to feel lost in the corporate shuffle.

Tomorrow, I am going out to Forks to visit Lake Pleasant Lumber. It should be a beautiful drive. Every time I drive the hour west from Port Angeles to Forks, I count the log trucks headed to town with their first load of logs of the day. Ninety percent of the logs come from Crown Z timberland. I place a tablet on the seat next to me and put a dot on the tablet for every loaded log truck that goes by. By the time I get to Forks there are typically 90-100 dots on the page. I think the highest count I ever had was 114.

When I got to the sawmill, the owner was not there so I talked with the plant manager and we walked through the mill. All he wanted to talk about was his sore shoulder and if I could help him since his wife was out of town for a week. I learned early on that the most important thing to do when any advance happens is to ignore what they're saying and stay focused on the business. It's all about the business…price, volume, production. After a couple of minutes, they get frustrated and get back to business. It works every time.

We have a couple of pals now, two chipmunks that live in the woods behind the house. They take sunflower seeds from our hands and are they cute! When they get their pouches full, one runs home by way of the wood pile and the other by way of a pile of bricks on the other side of the yard. They always take the same routes.

3/12/80

Last night we attended a dinner for the Northwest Timber Division in Port Angeles. The after-dinner music was provided by the Hurricane Ridge Runners, a great local group. The lead male singer works for Crown. Afterward, the Division Manager had a contest to see who could match up words commonly used by loggers with the right definition. It was quite funny. My boss was the only one to get all of them right.

LOGGER LINGO

1. _____Rainy weather, rainy country

2. _____Log rafting and storage area

3. _____Light summer underwear

4. _____A logging operation

5. _____Slit made by a saw

6. _____Crew bus7._____Logger's hero

8. _____High-water pants with no cuff or hem

9. _____A set of grasping jaws or pincers used in yarding operations

10. ____Company president or other high official

11. ____Snuff

12. ____A pile of logs stacked at a landing

13. ____West Coast Forester

14. ____Person who saws felled trees into log lengths

15. ____Hurry up

16. ____ Nose bag

17. ____Tractor mechanic

18.____Migratory logger

19. ____Signal man

20. ____Steel pegs in the soles of heavy boots to give loggers secure footing

21. ____Explosive-like spread of a forest fire due to weather conditions

22. ____Logging superintendent

23. ____Wire rope loop to grip logs being pulled to a landing

24. ____Latest year's height growth on a tree's main stem

25. ____Canada jay or whiskey jack

Possible answers:

Backfire	Boot jack
Camp robber	Choker
Fern hopper	High ball
Blow up	Brains
Cat doctor	Cold deck
Grapple	Kerf
Boom Bucker	Cat face
Crummy	Haywire
King Snipe	Dynamite
Hen skins	Boomer
Stag	Caulks
Leader	Bull of the woods
Show	Scaler
Tin pants	Whistle punk
Paul Bunyan's lunch pail	

Answers on page 85.

Paul Bunyan

69

4/15/80

On Saturday we flew around Mt. St. Helens and she is steaming and rumbling. Steam was flowing out of the side and the top of the cone, which is missing. Air traffic control placed air restrictions around the mountain: ten miles on the west side and twenty miles on the east side. The steam was flowing eastward. It was sunny and clear and we took about 30 slides with the telephoto lens. Mud flows created brown strips down the mountain making it look really dirty compared to the other snow-covered mountains.

So many sawmills are shut down or curtailed, we're buying all of the logs we can to chip up. We're in better shape than the mills in the Portland area. In fact, I've been able to share some of our chips with them by redirecting trucks on the south end of my area to the mills in the Columbia River. It seems like this bad market will last all summer. Many sawmills have written off 1980 and are looking to 1981 for any improvement. People say it is the worst market they have ever seen, since no one can see the light at the end of the tunnel.

The world pulp market is very, very strong so we don't even want to curtail production. Some pulp mills have cut back production due to a lack of chips. I have been lucky to work with a great supplier on Vancouver Island, Sooke Forest Products, and that has kept us going at Port Angeles.

Hershell Smith is the owner of Sooke and what a Scotsman. He can tell stories for hours. Every day is a great day for Hershell. Even though his sawmill is shut down, the chip prices are so high I've been able to buy several of his log rafts and he debarks and chips the logs for me. The chips are barged to Port Angeles and the bark to Port Townsend. It is such a lucrative agreement; every Friday morning he gets in his turboprop Super Goose airplane and flies to

Port Angeles with an invoice. At the airport, we have a drink in his plane, he gives me the invoice, and then he flies home. The Super Goose is a modernized twin-turbine version of the Grumman G-21 Goose and one beautiful airplane.

One of Hershell's stories that I'll always remember is when he bought a huge piece of land near Sea-Tac Airport years ago. Over time, the Sea-Tac Mall was built on one side of his property and office buildings on the other. All of the water drained from their parking lots onto his property, but he didn't know it because he lives in Canada. When he finally wanted to develop the property, he couldn't get a permit because now he owned a wetland and it had to be protected. Although he thought this was a crazy American law, we had a lot of laughs about it.

4/21/80

The 10% inflation and 19-20% interest rates are creating a depression for the northwest. We have started running portable chippers in the woods and some of our suppliers are chipping up their low-grade (utility and economy) lumber. A lot of logs are on the market because so many mills are down.

You would think the Timber Dept. wouldn't cut trees if they couldn't sell them for a profit, but they want to keep their people busy and meet their production numbers. We have been able to buy small sawlogs at a really good price and chip them up. It's crazy! It will all catch up with us by June 1st when the International Woodworkers Association (IWA), the sawmill and loggers union, is expected to go on strike, then no more logs. We are buying as many logs as possible in order to keep running. The IWA wants a one-year contract, which is also amazing, but the strategy is that their contract would then expire at the same time the pulp mill contracts do, giving them more leverage.

Last week, I flew up to Vancouver and took a seaplane out to a logging operation at Goliath Bay operated by Crown Canada. Mike Thompson, Crown's Fiber Manager, showed me around and explained the operation. The logs are yarded downhill to the facility and either tied together into log rafts for sale or chipped on site and loaded onto barges for pulp mills.

At the chipping plant, logs are debarked and chipped. The chips are blown onto one huge barge and hog fuel onto another. I'm buying only one barge of chips, because the barge is twice as large as the ones used in Puget Sound, and it may be difficult to unload.

Observing a Crown Canada chipping facility.

On Friday, I took the day off, and we went to Bremerton and toured the USS Missouri, thanks to a friendship I had with a woman whose husband was stationed on the ship. As we stepped on the ship, there was a tape of McArthur's voice at the surrendering ceremony playing over the loudspeaker. It must have been a bone-chilling experience to be on that destroyer during the war. I can really understand why men would be proud to serve on a ship like that.

Note: The USS Missouri was designed to be a fast battleship, a warship that balanced firepower and armor without sacrificing speed. *Missouri*'s 887'3" (270.4m) length accommodated four large engines with 212,000 shaft horsepower, allowing the battleship to hit speeds in excess of 33 knots, a significant improvement from the 27 knots of the previous class of battleship. In 1992, the battleship was decommissioned for a final time. In 1998, she opened her water-tight doors again as a historic museum.

5/4/80

We flew our plane down to see the latest changes in Mt. St. Helens. The top of the mountain had cracked open like an egg and the bulge on the north side was larger. Scientists predicted the mountain would blow to the north/northeast. Governor Dixie Lee Ray issued an evacuation order and it hopefully will save many lives. One landowner, Harry Truman, is defying the evacuation order and has become somewhat of a local celebrity.

5/18/80

Note: This is a day I will never forget, the day Mt. St. Helens blew. I wrote this after returning home from flying by the mountain during the eruption.

THE DAY THE MOUNTAIN BLEW
SUNDAY, MAY 18, 1980

On Sunday morning, we got up about 7:50 a.m. in our home in Sequim, Washington on the Olympic Peninsula, about 150 miles north of Mt. St. Helens.

8:40 We heard a sonic boom, then another and another. We went outside to see if we could understand what was going on. The booms continued at a rapid pace. The louder ones shook the windows and the house. The cows next door ran through the field. How many planes would it take to make so much noise? My pulse rate skyrocketed as I wondered if we were under attack from the Russians!

8:45 We called KIRO News Radio in Seattle to report the series of sonic booms. The reporter asked where we lived and how far Sequim was from Mt. St. Helens, then hung up.

8:48 KIRO reported on the radio that the mountain had erupted. A mushroom cloud of ash and smoke was billowing 50,000 feet high. The mountain is only 9,600 feet high!

9:00 We grabbed the camera and left for the airport. The weather was good. We only had eight pictures left on our roll of film.

9:45 We were flying toward Seattle and could see part of the mushroom cloud. Other clouds lay at the base of the mountain and high clouds blocked the top of the pillar of ash, but visibility was good. We could see the Olympic Mountains and Cascade Mountains clearly. We tuned into Flight Service on the airplane radio. A restricted zone was announced covering an area twenty miles west of the mountain and the whole eastern side wherever ash was present. The wind was blowing the ash over the Cascades in a path 80 miles wide. As we passed Mt. Rainier, we took a picture. It looked as though Rainier may be enveloped in ash at any moment, but it was just an illusion. The ash is moving behind the mountain into eastern Washington.

10:40 We passed into the area southwest of St. Helens and the air around the base of the mountain was clear. It looked like an atomic explosion – curling, bubbling smoke and ash towering in the sky. The blackened sky reminded us of a severe eastern thunderstorm. We saw lightning over the crater. Mt. Adams, to the southeast, which had looked pure white, was now blackened with ash. We took our last picture and were low on gas, so we headed to the Toledo, Washington airport to refuel. We landed, but no gas was available, so we took off for the Kelso/Longview airport. We were flying over the Toutle River and noticed how muddy it looked. Then we saw the logs – hundreds, no probably thousands of logs flowing down the river. Many looked fresh cuts as if they came out of a mill. Then we noticed Interstate 5, no traffic. Various intersections were jammed with cars, but traffic had been stopped. Then we saw why, the log flow was moving toward the I-5 bridge.

12:00 We landed at the Kelso airport, which was buzzing with activity. News crews from CBS, NBC and the Seattle Times had been flying in and out all morning. I offered to buy a roll of film from a reporter who was jamming a pack of a hundred rolls in his camera bag, but he refused. The state emergency team plans to use the hangers at the airport for people who must evacuate their homes. Two men in the airport office were verbally kicking themselves. They were flying near the mountain when she blew and had left their cameras at home. The girls at the counter started cooking hot dogs for the growing number of people flying in. A large Beech King Air, turbo prop, landed and taxied up to the office. Men in suits stepped off and then came Governor Dixie Lee Ray. She had been flying around the mountain to check on the devastation. She has been quite a governor.

1:00 Refueled, we took off from Kelso and flew above deserted I-5. It felt like we were in a movie--very strange! The log flow had passed under the I-5 bridge with no apparent damage and was heading toward the City of Castle Rock. As we got closer, the logs passed by the city and continued on to eventually meet the Columbia River in a few miles. At Kelso, we saw sail boats and pleasure boats tied up in the river, which would surely be swept away. Behind the log flow was a river of mud. Logs were strewn along the shores of the riverbed. Over the radio we heard Flight Service closing larger and larger areas around the mountain to all aircraft. There were helicopters below us, planes to the right and left and above us. The mountain continued to bubble and boil, like black towering cumulus clouds. We headed for home, still not believing what we had seen.

2:10 We landed at Diamond Point Airport and tied the plane down. We bought a six-pack of Bud from Dave at the airport store and told him what it was like. At home we heard over the radio that the ash was three inches thick in some eastern Washington towns and in Yakima, it was as black as night at noon. The ash was now reaching Spokane, 290 miles east of the mountain. Most eastern roads were closed as well as airports. In Packwood, Washington, the ash was so deep snow plows were clearing the roads. Many of the logs we saw charging down the Toutle River came from Weyerhaeuser's logging camp, which was completely wiped out. Now we are watching the news on TV to see what we saw, and help us fully comprehend the awesome power of the mountain.

5/26/80

Sunday, we woke up to the news of another eruption, but this time the wind blew the ash on Portland, Kelso and Longview. I-5 and a lot of other roads were closed. We spent most of the day listening to wind reports. Ash started coming up Hood Canal and by 6 p.m., we noticed ash on our car. It was very light and it built up in corners and along the edges of the windshield and felt really gritty.

In the Columbia River area, the ash was fairly deep and I am really concerned about what effect it will have on the pulp mill chip piles. I have been trying to get in touch with the Wauna chip buyer, but all of the phone lines are busy. The ferry system was really jammed at the news of ash in the area. The news a 4 p.m. said traffic was moving at 25-35 mph on I-5 from Olympia to Portland.

6/17/80

It has rained every day since May 19th. Ben is finally adjusting to the fact that the Toutle River is gone. It was a world-class fishing spot. We're going to put together a picture album of the Toutle after we get the latest shots of the mountain printed.

7/23/80

Greetings from Ashington! She did it again, and what an amazing sight. We were driving down Hood Canal towards Olympia when we heard it on the radio. We looked across the canal to see a huge white plume against a blue sky. Many people could see it this time, so it is now real to everyone. Everywhere people pulled off the road to watch. The wind was blowing northeast so Seattle didn't have to worry about ash.

A map of ash fallout across the country by the U. S. Geologic Survey

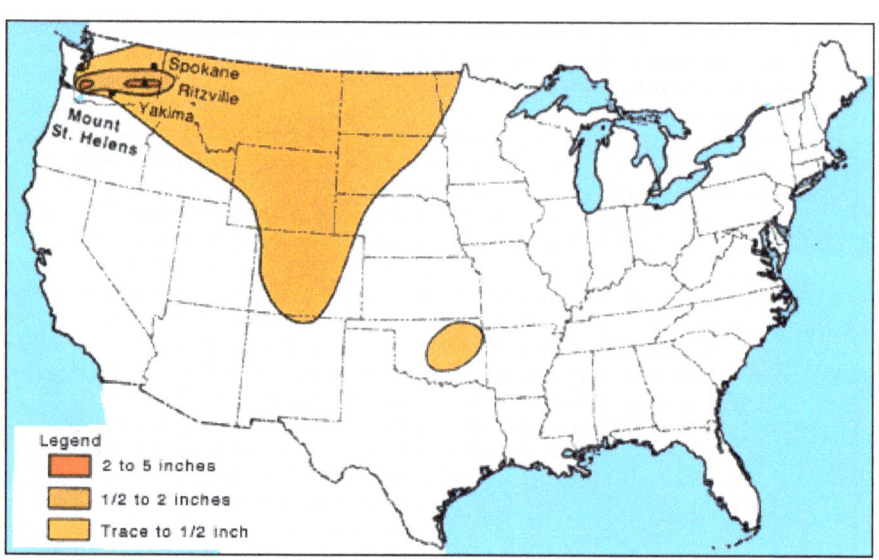

7/27/80

This new project I'm involved in is really interesting. It may be a bit confusing, but here goes. The U.S. Forest Service has been ordered to develop a management plan for each national forest. This order was included in the National Forest Management Act of 1976. It has taken the Forest Service this long to decide how to create the plan and what form it should take. Now, each forest is putting together an individual plan.

The rules of the planning process are that the Forest Service must ask for public input on what the important issues are, such as timber production, wildlife, recreation, etc. The rules also say that if the public, which includes Crown Z, does not take part in the process, then they cannot come back after the plan has been approved and say the Forest Service screwed up. It also says that any criticism of the plan after approval will only be accepted and reviewed on the subjects that we individually raise during the process. Therefore, Crown cannot criticize them on the issue of recreation if we do not talk to them about recreation during the process. Crown has always been a quiet company, staying out of the limelight and avoiding many hassles from preservationists, so this presents a challenge.

At a meeting in Portland recently, two VPs spoke and said we must get involved. We must speak out and anything we say will be backed by the company. That's a first! Traditionally, Crown forbids anyone to speak for the company without approval from San Francisco. So, various people were chosen to be Crown representatives of the national forests.

I've been assigned to cover the Olympic National Forest and Mt. Baker National Forest. We were directed to meet with the Forest Service's team of specialists, get to know them, go to their meetings, and keep tabs on how the process is working. We will write letters to them stressing our opinions on different issues. Also, we will talk to the people in the lumber industry, union leaders, and anyone who could be affected by a change in Forest Service policy.

The one policy that we are concerned about is the allowable cut of timber on national forest land. A drop in the "allowable cut" will decrease lumber supply and increase prices, create fewer jobs, fewer chips for the pulp mills, and raise chip prices. Special interest groups are also very aware of this planning process. The Sierra Club has a lot of people involved.

We are all for multiple-use management of our forests, but we all have special interests. Ours is for sustained-yield forestry, where timber growing and harvesting is economical. Sustained yield means only cutting enough every year so that there will be the same volume of trees cut each year in perpetuity. Makes sense to me, yet it's a highly controversial matter. Some people think it's wrong, but it's definitely better than the old 'cut and run' method, which I've seen plenty of around here.

This should be really interesting since I will meet a lot of new people in industry and government, but all of this has to be done in my spare time, because my regular job continues. The regular job is easing up since the lumber market has improved and sawmills are back to two and three shifts. What a relief! I'm very optimistic about the next nine months.

7/28/80

Just got back from flying over Mt. St. Helens. It was just shocking. Last week's eruption was the first one that could be seen by most people. It was a clear day and the plume was white against the blue sky. Scientists say this may go on for years.

In this photo it looks so sad.

Tomorrow both pulp mills and the Timber Department are competing in a softball tournament. I was drafted to play on the Timber team. It's salaried people only. Someone created Timber Beast t-shirts, and we'll wear orange Crown Z suspenders and orange hats. The Port Angeles mill is buying beer for all players and spectators, so it should be fun.

10/27/80

This is the first letter I've written since your visit. I better get back in the swing of things since Christmas cards aren't far away. I've had to be on the road a lot lately, which included attending a seminar on "The Art of Negotiating," which was really good.

Did you hear the mountain blew again two weeks ago? It was another big blast with a pyroclastic flow. It was preceded by harmonic tremors and the area around the mountain was evacuated. Weyerhaeuser has over five hundred loggers working near the mountain recovering the downed trees.

The lumber market is in another downturn, the dreaded double dip. Sawmills are curtailing and about all logging on the peninsula has stopped. We don't see any signs of recovery until June next year when it will be a slow buildup of production. We are not expecting to see normal production levels until April 1982. The sawmill managers I talk to have never seen the market in such bad shape. Of course, this makes the pulp mills very nervous, because most of the chip supply comes from sawmills. Last year we went through the same cycle, but there was an initial recovery in the spring. Now, no one is sure when it will recover. I couldn't have asked for a more unique learning experience.

We had some excitement last Thursday. Crown had a slash burn that got out of control. Slash is the limbs and brush left after a logging operation. It's burned to prepare the ground for replanting and prevents wildfires from escalating. Anyway, the person in charge of what should have been a controlled burn made a bad judgment. The wind picked up to thirty knots and took the fire up the side of the hill.

As I was driving through Discovery Bay listening to my company radio, the timber office was having trouble getting food to the fire line, so I called in and took care of getting sandwiches, chips, and soda and delivered the goods to them.

The fire was so out of control that I couldn't stay home knowing what was going on, so I went to the Timber office and made myself available to help. The Timber Dept. has a fire plan for any emergency. All people take their assigned places, so I could only help with odd jobs. I made phone calls, sandwiches, and coffee and helped keep the atmosphere at the control center light when things got heavy.

The fire spread so fast that cats had to be brought in from the west end of the peninsula. It was incredible how much equipment was put on that hill. The wind blew the flames and sparks hundreds of feet. It looked like a blowtorch on the mountain. At 1 a.m. the fire was totally out of control and with the high winds there wasn't much that could be done. A skeleton crew was left on the hill and the rest sent home to get some sleep. The next morning sixty people were up there firefighting, and the wind didn't let up. It was late Saturday before the fire was under control.

Today, Monday, the crews are still mopping up, completely putting out the spots anywhere where the ground is hot. That includes digging up smoldering tree roots. The fire burned forty-three acres, which isn't very big on the scale of forest fires, but it was really big for all of us.

Last Tuesday, we were invited to an open house at Foss Launch and Tug Company in Seattle. Foss tows all of our chip barges in Puget Sound. They were showing off a new tugboat. Next to it was the Thea Foss, the old Lionel Barrymore yacht that had two bars open and hot snacks. The new tug is a beauty and is faster than the ones they've been using to tow our barges.

11/23/80

Remember I said my boss, Don Hansen, accepted the chip buyer's job in California? Last week his boss, Brownie, was here and I thought I would find out who my new boss was. Instead, Brownie asked me to pick up Don's duties saying it shouldn't be any big deal! That means taking total responsibility and authority in Puget Sound for $28-30 million worth of fiber purchases each year for these mills. At first it sounded great, but it's more work at a higher level and I would have to ignore important work I'm now doing or work longer hours than my current ten to twelve hours/day.

I told Brownie it wouldn't work and he didn't appreciate that. What really made me mad was that I wouldn't get any grades or pay increases. I said I would put together a letter of recommendation for how the job should be set up. I typed it up and it calls for a full-time assistant and part-time secretary. Brownie won't like it, but I feel that's how it has to be. He won't have time to discuss it until after Thanksgiving.

ANSWERS TO LOGGER LINGO:

1) Tin pants show. 2) Boom. 3) Hen skins. 4) Show. 5) Kerf. 6) Crummy. 7) Paul Bunyan. 8) Stag. 9) Grapple. 10) Brains. 11) Dynamite. 12) Cold deck. 13) Fern hopper. 14) Bucker. 15) Hi ball. 16) Paul Bunyan's lunch pail. 17) Cat doctor. 18) Boomer. 19) Whistle punk. 20) Caulks. 21) Blow up. 22) Bull of the Woods. 23) Choker. 24) Leader. 25) Camp robber.

1981

1/11/81

Last week, I had to spend Monday and Tuesday in Vancouver, BC. I was scheduled to fly, but SeaTac was fogged in and no flights were leaving, so I drove. I stayed at a hotel called the Four Seasons. It cost $69 for a single…expensive, but really nice. My boss, Brownie, was up there also. We had a dinner meeting and then a morning meeting with the managers of Crown Canada's Wood Fibre Supply.

Tuesday, I drove to Portland and crashed a Columbia River chip buyer meeting in the Portland office. Since I now have the authority, I do what I think is best and don't have to ask anyone. I didn't get a warm welcome from the other supervisor, but we did get into some good discussions, and I proved a little more that our areas overlap and that sharing information is very important.

Since I have help at work now, I've been able to do things that I put off for months. I only asked for one assistant, and now I have three! Brownie was very slick to make this happen. His timber people don't have much to do since the tree farm is shut down until March. Other managers were also laying off people. The three people worked under Brownie, so all of a sudden, he recognized that I could easily keep them busy and not subject to layoff.

I've got Mary doing bookwork, posting information, filing, and writing reports. Mac does all of the day-to-day scheduling, forecasting and problem-solving. Marvin works on our hog fuel shortage. He is getting special projects running that I have been preparing for months, yet didn't have the time to put into action. We're accomplishing a lot. It's like a totally different job that's now being done the way it should have been all along. Of course, Portland doesn't seem to care about what we're accomplishing, but I do, and that's all that matters.

As I get this backlog of projects cleaned up, it'll give me more time to get involved in the National Forest planning process. Remember I am working with the Olympic and Mt. Baker National Forests on their plans? There are twelve people in Crown assigned to monitor the different forests. It's the largest planning process ever attempted. We are trying to make sure that commercial forest land doesn't end up being converted to other protected uses. There are a lot of uses that coexist with timber management, but environmentalists really want to stop cutting all trees. They start with preserving old trees, then plants, then owls, then elk, then water, then historical spots such as old trapper cabins and trails, and all of a sudden there's not much land available for harvesting trees, and it results in fewer wood products, which results in higher prices for us.

1/18/81

On Thursday and Friday, I attended a seminar on "Biomass for Energy" that was put on by a fellow I have worked with occasionally this past year to find the best way to hog up logging slash and sorting yard waste, which is a new idea. This guy got hooked up with an equipment manufacturer and a distribution/sales organization for his new invention, a solid waste demolisher. He is promoting the ability to use log yard waste for energy and had 30 speakers at the seminar sharing current research on the subject. Those who spoke were from the US Dept. of Energy, EPA, Bonneville Power, equipment manufacturers, and sawmill owners. It was the first seminar of its type and everyone requested that it be an annual event.

2/8/81

Last weekend I spent most of my time writing a presentation for our department reorganization. About a month ago, it was announced that our department would be consolidated with three other purchasing departments: logs, stumpage and land, and it would be headed by an unidentified person that we started calling Mr. X.

I talked to both of my pulp mill managers about the qualifications for that job. At Port Townsend, the manager said that Mr. X should have years of experience and be good at conceptualizing and that I definitely did not have the credibility to do the job. At Port Angeles, he said all it should take is good communication skills, organization and imagination and he would gladly be a reference for me since we have worked closely on some special projects. He also said our department was in such bad shape it couldn't get any worse. That gave me the confidence to call Vice President Carlson and inquire about the job. He invited me to come to his office in Portland and talk to him about it, so last Tuesday, I did.

Crown is going through a lot of reorganization and is pulling in its horns in many areas. I figured I had nothing to lose by talking to Carlson. I put together a seven-page presentation that included a four-step proposal for reorganization with the "how" and "why" of each and then presented my qualifications for the top job.

The presentation went really well, and I spent an hour and a half with the VP. He was an excellent listener and asked many questions. He outlined his idea of the job and its scope was twice as large as what had been announced, so my chances are slim, but now he has a very different impression of who I am and what I'm looking for.

Brownie was not pleased that I called on the VP, but I gave him a copy of the presentation, and he did just what I expected-- dismissed it as insignificant and immediately threw it in the trash. He does not take me seriously, and that is a problem, but I'm trying to work around it.

My assistants are doing a great job and I have been able to address the larger issues facing the mills. As the lumber market bottoms out, we expect a very slow recovery by mid-year, just when it is again time for labor negotiations. Remember when I was on strike duty? It could happen again this summer. We are also faced with the threat that the Canadian sawmills and pulp mills might go on strike, so it promises to be a very wild summer.

I am very involved with the National Forest planning process, especially in the Olympic National Forest. On Tuesday, I fly to Portland and meet with the regional planning group. A lot of land is going to be tied up in the national forests for spotted owls and wild and scenic rivers. The industry is not cohesive enough to fight the preservationists on these issues, but I and others on the task force are presenting our views anyway. The Olympic National Forest plans to manage forty-four pairs of spotted owls. Their specialists believe that each pair needs 810 acres to live on…all below 1500' elevation on prime commercial forest land! It couldn't be a coincidence, could it?

3/19/81

It has been so busy, I haven't written due to lack of energy. On Saturday, I was almost too tired to move. Three weeks ago, Brownie, my boss, arranged a formal meeting with the President of Pulp & Paper, whose responsibility includes the two mills I serve. The meeting was to be held at the Port Ludlow resort, about forty minutes from here. Brownie scheduled it for one and a half days and sixteen people were mandated to attend. The goal was to share information so he could better understand the profit picture for the two pulp mills, while we explained to him how Fiber Supply operates.

A few days before the meeting, Brownie said since I know the most about this area that I should handle our part of the meeting. I put my assistants to work gathering information and making individual binders with separators for the eleven topics I wanted to cover, which included about sixty-five pages of handouts.

The resort was very fancy, so I wore my business jacket and a skirt. The rooms were pretty expensive, so everyone doubled up. I was with the other female in the group, Diane Perry, who was recently assigned the job of closing down our Clallam Bay Tree Farm on the peninsula by year's end. It's a really tough job, but she is a tough lady. She is about thirty-five and her nickname is "The Dragon Lady." She is really nice, but very political. I have to watch what I say around her. Some people at Crown spend more time playing politics than working. If she does a good job closing down the tree farm, I'm sure she'll go on to bigger and better things.

The agenda for the meeting was:

Monday

- Luncheon Noon-1 p.m.

- Presentation by Port Townsend Mill Management   1-5 p.m.

Tuesday:

- Presentation by Port Angeles Mill Management 8 a.m. to noon

- Presentation by Puget Sound Wood Fiber Supply (me) 1-5 p.m.

Well, each pulp mill talked for about one hour and that was it. Port Townsend was done by 2:00 and Port Angeles was done by 3:00, and they thought the meeting would be over.

They have great disdain for Fiber Supply because they don't control it, so I guess this was their way to cut this lengthy meeting down considerably. Everyone figured I would never have enough to talk about, but none of them really ever took the time to understand what I did. So, without a pause in the program, I jumped right in and began my presentation at 3:15 p.m. on the first day.

I had separated Fiber Supply's job in Puget Sound into eleven subjects and put the high points of each topic on a chart board, which I used to talk from, then gave out the handouts at the end of each topic. It apparently went over really well, because the mill management teams jumped into a lot of discussion about each subject and questions that were not always very pleasant to answer.

We paused at 5 p.m. and continued at 8 a.m. the next day. We ended up with a list of twenty-three subjects the group thought should be analyzed and the appropriate people were assigned to each one. I ended up with seven new tasks. The discussions were so good, the meeting didn't end until late afternoon that day.

Two of the people at the meeting were from Crown Canada's Fibre Supply Department in Vancouver, Phil Musgrave and Mike Thompson. I personally invited them and am I glad. We depend on them so much at Port Angeles and they were the best people to answer the heavy questions that came up about the Canadian chip market. It worked out well because they witnessed first-hand what length my pulp mill managers try to get involved in Fiber Supply. In Canada, the Fiber Supply Department is left alone because they are completely trusted. Down here, Fiber Supply Management in Portland is so mistrusted that there is a constant fight for either undermining or controlling the department. Regardless, the meeting was highly successful, at least for our department.

Last Friday. George Pearson, the head of all Canadian operations was promoted to Senior VP for U.S. Timber and Wood Products, which means my department reports to him through the long chain of command. Phil Musgrave, Canadian Fiber Supply, reports directly to Pearson. I found out that after our Port Ludlow meeting, Pearson bent Phil's ear for an hour trying to find out how well we all got along. Phil and I work well together and he thinks I am the only sane one in our group. It's funny how things work out. Mike Thompson said Pearson has been given the U.S. operations to be a hatchet man and get this place straightened out. Hallelujah!

Last Thursday and Friday I had to go to Portland for a couple of meetings. I took a flight out of Port Angeles at 6:30 a.m., but en route, the pilot got word that SeaTac was fogged in so we landed at Bremerton and waited for two hours. When we finally got into SeaTac, I missed my flight to Portland and had to wait two more hours. I finally arrived at the office at 1:15 p.m., missing four hours of an all-day meeting. As they say, we can never be in a real hurry living on the peninsula. If it isn't fogged in flights, it's late ferries or a hundred of campers sightseeing along Hood Canal.

When the plane was finally ready to take off for Portland, the only seats left were in first class, so I got a taste of real airline service. The ticket cost $11 more and included one free drink. Just a bit expensive! The seats were very comfortable and roomy, and the stewardess did hang up my coat, which was nice. The weather was crystal clear so I had an excellent view of Mt. St. Helens.

I had a nice surprise when I was in Portland, Brownie gave me a raise. It wasn't large, but every bit counts. All of the work for that meeting at Port Ludlow was worth it. Brownie is really a very nice person. He is only two years away from retirement and he just isn't interested in Fiber Supply because it is so complex and constantly changing. He can hardly wait for Mr. X to appear so he can disappear. Brownie said they continue interviewing for Mr. X, and we should have him within a month. He expects it to be a pulp and paper man from back east. Great. He'll be the head of a department and won't have the foggiest idea what Fiber Supply is all about. Brownie thinks it will take him at least 9-12 months to get his feet on the ground.

Remember I said I roomed with Diane at the Port Ludlow meeting? She asked me dozens of questions about Fiber Supply in the morning since she didn't know anything about it either. I mentioned to her that I had made a presentation to VP Carlson and she was really impressed. I am sure she will check that out since no one does things like that. I'm working on another proposal that I hope to have ready for Mr. X. and I plan to run it by the pulp mill managers first to get their approval and perhaps give it a little extra support.

Well, this week was almost as crazy as last week. Monday morning started with a tugboat strike in Puget Sound. No chip barges are moving and probably won't for three to four weeks, from the looks of things. It took even the tug companies by surprise, so at the moment I have chips moving all over Puget Sound in trucks. It's all working out well much to the surprise of Portland chip buyers and managers who think only they have the ability to solve a crisis. The range of personalities and egos in this corporation is incredible. What a lesson in humanity.

A tugboat in Elliott Bay in Seattle

6/8/81

When we returned home from vacation our grass was at least one foot tall, so it must have rained a lot while we were gone. The new neighbors, Steve and Dan, are foresters and they surprised us by putting in a 10'x10' garden in our side yard with tomato plants! What a surprise! They bought two ducks while we were gone, let them into our pond area, and asked us to feed them while they're firefighting this summer.

Reinhard has gotten attached to the ducks and takes them for a walk around the property every day. They really squawk when he walks too fast and waddle right after him. Their names are Thanksgiving and Christmas, which gives you an idea of what lies ahead! This is Christmas and she is a bit of a slowpoke.

7/6/81

Our department reorganization is going slowly. I heard the top job was offered to three different people, and they all turned it down. I don't blame someone who has really made a name for themselves and is asked to take this job. Who would want to take on a hugely complex department with a good chance of failure? It's all up in the air. My boss has already removed himself from our group's functions.

One thing we know is that we will report to a Pulp & Paper person in San Francisco instead of the VP of Timber. Also, the Chip Buyer for the Columbia River was asked to leave because he screwed something up badly. I'm not sure what it was. Luckily, he is sixty-two and was allowed to take early retirement. Some people expect our controller to get the ax next. All this makes people very nervous and some are grasping for all the power they can get. It is really fascinating. I'm in an isolated position, which is good, so I have nothing to worry about.

Ben and Diane came over for four days the week before July 4th. As they brought things into the house, Diane was carrying a gallon of red wine and a freak thing happened. Her arms were full and as she reached to put the wine on the kitchen counter, she hit the edge of the counter about a half inch from the bottom of the jug and the whole bottom of that gallon jug cracked and fell off. Instantly, we had red wine running all over the kitchen carpet! We were laughing hysterically and reaching for every towel we could find. Luckily, the carpet cleaned up beautifully, and we had a full load of wine-soaked towels to wash.

7/15/81

This week, the sawmills went on strike in British Columbia, and their pulp mills may also go out very soon. I have really been busy making alternate arrangements for chips. I have a stockpile at each mill that will easily carry us six weeks, but rumors say it could last ten weeks. I am looking at various alternatives, just in case. All day long, it was like a giant mystery unfolding as things went from bad to worse. I got calls from people wanting to sell me chips at far from bargain prices.

7/20/81

Press release: Today, Crown Zellerbach announced the formation of a new Wood Fiber Supply Group to be based in Portland, Oregon. This new group will report to Pulp and Paper Management and will provide close coordination of the planning, strategy, and implementation necessary to optimize the fiber supply required for the corporation's Northwest Pulp and Paper operations.

Named as Fiber Supply Manager is A. H. Stebbins, formerly Manager of Treated Wood Products, Gulfport, Mississippi. Mr. Stebbins will report to R. L. Appling, Vice President of Pulp and Paper, SFO. Art Stebbins will assume his new duties approximately September 1st.

Management members of the new group include R. E. Breuner, Planning Manager; R. R. Fay, Manager Fiber Demand; Frank Misa, Chip Supervisor Columbia River; Mary Schroeder, Chip Supervisor Puget Sound; and James Paschall, Log Buying Supervisor.

8/3/81

The department reorganization finally took place and I'm still here. Now I am the Fiber Supply Supervisor for Puget Sound. It is a higher pay grade, but I don't know if I get a raise. Until our new manager comes on line everything is in a holding pattern. Mac McInnes in Port Angeles now reports to me and is not so sure he likes the idea of being in Pulp & Paper. He has been doing the same job for the Timber Department for many years. Now he works in the hectic world of fiber supply. He's fifty-eight years old and does a good job. This weekend is time for the Timber Dept. picnic again with crab, clams, salmon, and oysters. I can hardly wait!

The pulp log group in the Timber Department is now under Pulp & Paper, but at least we, the fiber supply folks, do not report to the pulp mill managers. The pulp mills only plan out as far as their order file, which sometimes is only two months. If they imposed their will on fiber supply, it would mean short term agreements and results totally incompatible with the cyclic nature of the lumber business.

9/1/81

At work, the Canadian sawmill strike is now over, but because the lumber market is so bad, some are curtailing, but many of the sawmills did not start up. The poor market is hitting Crown Z very hard. Many people are being let go and older employees, who can take early retirement, will be next. Any excess travel is cut and everyone is asked to let their boss know what costs can be eliminated. The pulp mills are under severe pressure to make a dollar wherever possible. They look to me to cut chip prices since I am almost fifty percent of the mill's total costs. It should be interesting.

Today, I took the Port Townsend pulp mill manager and controller to see the whole log chipping operation. It took almost half of the day, so I brought along box lunches. Two Timber Department people also went along to explain what was going on at the site. Our new Fiber Supply Department head starts work on September 14th, so I will be going to Portland that week to meet with him. I have heard a lot of good things about him; the most important quality is that he is a real people person. Our department needs that badly, so things are looking up.

10/5/81

The state of the economy is having a devastating effect on the Northwest lumber industry. There is no end in sight. Most people are resigned to wait until the spring of 1983 to make a profit again. I'm thinking that many mills will go out of business for good.

Remember I told you about my new boss, Art Stebbins? He came for a three-day visit last week and brought his boss, Bob

Appling, the VP of Pulp and Paper. It was very short notice, but everything worked out fine.

They arrived Monday afternoon, and I took them into the woods to see our chipping operations. It was a nasty day, and thank goodness they brought along rain gear and boots. It just poured as we watched the crew chip up whole trees and blow the chips into a van. We visited two different logging operations and then went to the sorting yard, which took up the afternoon, and then we met for dinner.

I had taken my dinner clothes to the pulp mill, so when I dropped them off at the motel, I went to the mill to change. The timber managers and pulp mill management team met us for dinner at Manresa Castle. The Tree Farm Manager, Diane, was with us that evening.

I was a little unsure what to think of Art and Bob, but the ice cracked while we were all having a cocktail before dinner. The Assistant Pulp Mill Manager (who is on my list of irritating people) said, "It sure is different to have two women with us this evening." to which Appling replied, "I wonder when we're going to have a female pulp mill manager?" and he continued "I think I'll make it my special project before I retire (he is 58) to see we have a female manager," at which point everyone shut up. I just loved it!

The next day, I took them to one of my large suppliers to meet the managers and see the mill. We ended up back at Port Townsend for lunch with mill management. The mill is on a real austerity program, so instead of taking everyone out to lunch, I had lunch brought in from my favorite deli, Waddycallit. The mill people were absolute shocked that I would do that for a VP. During the lunch, Appling said it was real good, and his boss would have enjoyed it. Chalk up one point.

After the lunch, the mill manager (who is typically a pontificator) was laying a real thick coat on his presentation about the mill operations when Appling interrupted and said, "That's a bunch of bullshit!" He's absolutely just what my department needed, someone high enough to cut through the fat and get to the meat of an issue. Immediately, I had a lot of respect for the guy.

The next day, I drove them to Port Angeles to check into another motel. Again, I went to the pulp mill to change clothes and then pick them up for dinner with mill management. Dinner went along beautifully until the end, when Art was looking totally drained and dead tired. He was overloaded with information and hadn't relaxed since they arrived. He looked over at me and said, "Mary, isn't it time to tuck your bosses in?" At which point the pulp mill people were saying things like, "I didn't know that was in your job description, ha, ha, ha." Appling quietly said "I saw a good corporate movie last week on sexual harassment." And again, everyone shut up as if someone snapped their fingers. It was great!

When I dropped them off at the motel, Appling said, "Mary, when you pick us up in the morning, I want you to park in a different spot. I want to be sure you went home!" It all went like clockwork and I guess it impressed him a lot. In the morning, I picked them up at 7:30, and we toured the city and then the Port Angeles pulp mill at 8:00.

I had another supplier meeting scheduled for them for 10 a.m. We were chatting with the pulp mill management as the clock ticked 9:55, 56, 57, and I got out my keys and finally stood up and said we have to go, when Appling said, "Yes, Mother." He said it in a very positive and friendly way, so now I have a new nickname.

Later he asked me if it helped to be a woman in this job. I told him that it probably helped, because I can convey to the mills that I really care about their problems and I have less of a tendency to use a power play. When I put them on the plane home, I felt as positive as I have ever felt in this job in two years.

November 1981

A big storm came through here today and did it blow! The floating bridges in Seattle were closed as winds gusted 50 mph. We heard the wind early in the morning, so we packed a lunch and headed to the clubhouse. The club is a small old house on the port property in Sequim Bay, so we could see the waves crashing and logs being thrown up on the beach. The dock where Don and Chuck's boats were tied up was pointed north instead of east, and the anchor chain snapped, so we called them. The next thing we knew, we had a party going at the club. I went to the store and got fixings for chili and baked a couple of apple pies.

Sequim Bay

Reinhard is vice commodore of the Sequim Bay Yacht Club, which means whenever the commodore can't be at a meeting, he runs it. He ran the last two and did a splendid job. We have a lot of retired people in the club, and all of the ladies love him. He is also the official barkeep, so he's very popular. He got people interested in paneling the inside of the clubhouse with cedar boards to cover up the old wallpaper. The guys had a lot of energy left, so they made some boards for the wall out of cedar from Butchers pole yard. One of the club members had a table saw, and out of a slab from Butchers, we can get one beautiful board of cedar. Another member donated an old wood stove. It was all rusty, so a few guys sanded and repainted it. Someone donated brick for a base and the club approved the purchase of a pipe to vent the smoke. So now, instead of buying oil for the furnace, we can heat the club with beach wood.

Two weeks ago, the marketing manager of Foss Launch & Tug, which tows all of our chip barges in Puget Sound, invited us to the University of Washington stadium to watch the Huskies and Stanford game. Our trip to the stadium was a lot of fun on their entertainment boat, Thea Foss. There were about 80 people on board to make the trip from the Foss dock to the university on Lake Washington, a 45-minute cruise. Our seats were on the 49-yard line on the Husky side.

The yacht club had a special board meeting this week to plan fora good turnout at the Port of Port Angeles public hearing to change the Port's comprehensive plan to include the marina at Sequim Bay. We had collected over two hundred signatures on a petition asking that they go ahead with the marina.

11/29/81

Happy Thanksgiving! Today we spent some time at the clubhouse and christened the wood stove with its first load of wood. After we had been home awhile, Reinhard went back to the club to check the stove to be sure the fire was out. He found a mother cat and two kittens on the porch. One of the little ones was so friendly, he called and asked if I wanted it. It's about 8" long and looks to be about 10-12 weeks old. Its hair is about 1 ½" long and has a rusty color. It has the biggest round eyes I've ever seen and a purr that sounds like a diesel truck.

12/7/81

We've had Ginger for a week now and what a treat. Reinhard calls her Screwball, since she goes crazy running from one room to another, jumping and tumbling at the slightest noise or movement. Then she practically passes out on his lap. She is so small, she loves to crawl onto one of our shoulders and tries to lie down. She's gold, cream and tan with a white belly and paws. The hair around her neck is the longest giving her a lion look. She has two little black dots on her nose and it looks like someone used a magic marker or felt pen on her. Reinhard has never had a kitten so he is amazed at her energy and playfulness. He asked how long this would last and I assured him in a couple of months she would be a lot calmer, I hope.

Our neighbors are back from firefighting, so we gave them back their ducks minus two that we kept. The challenge is training them to live at their house. We put food on the trail and keep moving it a few feet every day. The ducks follow the food and fly right back to the pond. If their ducks aren't living at their house by fall, they're going to be our dinner…just kidding.

12/29/81

Yesterday, I made a beef roast with dumplings German style. While we were eating, we put Ginger on the porch. All of a sudden, we saw that she was holding up one back leg and it looked like she was dripping blood. I ran to pick her up and she was covered with red wine! She jumped in Reinhard's bucket of fermenting wine. What a mess. She licked it all off and had a good sound sleep.

She's been doing so well, not touching the Christmas tree, plants or jumping on the kitchen table until this morning while I was in the shower. When I got out, six balls from our tree were scattered from the kitchen to the basement. She must have moved fast since it seemed like I was only out of the room for five minutes.

Later, when Reinhard found her, she was half way up the tree. We'll take it down tonight. She also loves paper, and right now, she is rolling around the kitchen floor in a paper bag. Cheap thrills!

1982

1/6/82

Sequim has a total of 12" of snow and Port Angeles has 16". What a surprise! I'm scheduled to get studded tires tomorrow if I can make it to the service station.

Things have been pretty slow at work this month, but are starting to pick up this week. I was notified that I might have a barge strike on my hands in two weeks, which is just what we need.

Last Friday I had to be in Seattle for two events. In the morning was the unveiling of the world's largest chipper. It was manufactured in Seattle, and a special demonstration was held by invitation only. There were about 150 people there and lunch was served in between demonstrations.

Remember Diane Perry, the lady who is the new tree farm manager for Puget Sound? She was there also. She doesn't know much about the equipment or what to expect at a demo like this. I talked to her afterward and all she could say was, "It wasn't like Boeing unveiling their new airplane." Really! A week earlier, Boeing had an exhibition that cost thousands to show off a new airplane.

Well, this chipper demo was at a manufacturing plant. It was cold and rainy, so we all stood in the doorway of the plant while the chipper operated outside. After every test load of material fed through the chipper, we all marched out in the rain with little plastic bags to pick up samples. The wind was blowing, and everyone was quite cold.

Lunch was good, but it didn't do much to warm us up. After four hours, my legs were shaking, so I left. Diane and I ended up going back on the same ferry, so I sat with her in the restaurant. She was at a loss for words at this new experience. Apparently, it just wasn't her style.

That evening, I met with three people from my department. We had dinner with a chip buyer from a competing firm that we often sell wood waste to. It was contract renewal time. We had dinner in a very nice restaurant where I had a small filet mignon for $19! I couldn't believe how expensive that was!

I'm happy to announce Reinhard was elected Commodore of our yacht club. We are both looking forward to a fun year in the club. The Sequim Bay Marina has been approved, but due to high interest rates, it may not be constructed until sometime in 1983. It will have over five hundred dock spaces, which are badly needed in this area.

Other exciting news is that one of our ducks has laid seven eggs and I doubt they will become dinner since they really are pets.

2/22/82

My best suppliers (and the most stable ones) are finally shutting down because of the bad lumber market. One told me last week that the price of studs finally reached the price it was in 1962. The mills that are the most efficient and even have their own log supply cannot hang on any longer. Now, I'm very glad we purchased the extra volume in December. I thought this would happen in January, so I wasn't off by much. The main concern now is hog fuel. We have lost 60% of our supply because of sawmill shutdowns. That is very hard to make up. Both pulp mills want updates daily on how I'm doing. Never a dull moment.

I had an interesting experience last Friday. Crown is trying to sell the Port Townsend mill and a Japanese firm is considering buying it. I was asked to put together information on wood supply and be at the mill on Friday, in case they needed more information. The Assistant Mill Manager asked me if I had enough time to take one of the Japanese out to see our portable chipping operation, because the man didn't have anything to do for a few hours. The hitch was he didn't speak any English. No problem—we took off and I found out he did know "Douglas fir" and "truck" and later "chipping machine." It turned out he was their company's forest manager.

We pulled up to the chipper in an area 6" deep in mud. I was barely out of the car and he was leaping across the site and around the semi that was being loaded. By the time I caught up with him, he was standing right in line with reject material that's kicked out of the side of the chipper with great force. All I could think was him getting an eye knocked out. I was glad the machine operator realized what was happening and shut it down when he saw me waving frantically to get the man away from the area. At times like that, the language gap is really a mile wide.

Next, I stopped at the Crown Timber office to get directions to another woods chipper, which is frequently moved to different logging sites. Dale, a female forester, gave me directions. The gentleman was totally enthralled with Dale, who is 5'8" with beautiful long blonde hair. It must have been very confusing to him to have two women showing him around the woods. The tour was a success and I was asked to join the group for lunch, so 16 of us ate at the Sea Galley restaurant. Afterwards, I met with two of their team and an interpreter to discuss our wood supply.

3/4/82

On Tuesday, I had to go to Portland and submit my PIA – Profit Improvement Action Plan, KRP – Key Results Management Plan, and PRIDE – Personnel Resources Identification and Development Plan. My PIAs and KRPs were approved, so I had no problem with that, but this was the first year for PRIDE. It's a process where my boss fills out the form about me. Then he attends a roundtable meeting in San Francisco with his peers and boss where each person reads the PRIDE reports on the people immediately under him.

The form includes past experience, present job, personal strengths, developmental needs (weaknesses phrased nicely), and a plan to overcome those needs, then possible career paths. I had to put one together for myself and my boss, Art, put one together for me, on everything except past experience.

I had a hard time answering the career path section, so I talked to both mill managers and two people in my department in Portland, whose opinion I value. Art and I went through both our forms to combine and rearrange it and come up with a final product he would take to San Francisco. Among the strengths he listed for me are the ability to handle a lot of pressure, being highly organized, resilient, and good at short- range planning. The three weaknesses were: 1) the need to improve my relationship with the Timber Manger (the Dragon Lady, Diane), 2) to be more assertive with the pulp mill managers, and 3) the need to have more technical knowledge about the inner workings of the pulp mills. For three weaknesses, those weren't too bad really. He had eight strengths listed, so I think it balanced out well.

For the first two weaknesses, I have to work those out myself. Third, I plan to spend three days between now and the end of the year at each mill working with the paper machine superintendent, pulp mill superintendent, and technical department. I worked on my relationship with Diane this afternoon—we spent three hours going over my Key Results Program. I thought if I shared my goals with her, it might open up a dialogue, since I depend on her for chips. I also told her Art's opinion that I must improve our relationship. She agreed we have been having problems, and then she told me her problems and she has a lot of them! Besides taking over a tree farm that this year will be lucky to make a profit, she has all new people under her who have been given new job titles, who can't seem to get along with one another, who depend on her for guidance, and she has never run a tree farm before.

Her boss, the VP of Timber, is on her back every day for answers, but the ones she gives him after he finds out the answers are wrong. Then she goes home and her kids are crying because they were previously in a high-tech school and don't like Port Townsend. Then I finish off her day by calling and asking if I can change their production schedule. Holy cow, it seems like she's in a tough position she wasn't prepared for. She said if she had it to do all over again, she would never have taken the job. She worked real hard in Portland to become the Timber VP's favorite, and now she's paying the price.

I met with the Port Angeles mill manager today and also reviewed my PIAs and KRPs, etc. and told him that Art felt one of my weaknesses was the need to be more assertive. He said he thought I did just fine in that area and that most men think all women need to be more assertive—a very good point.

The section about career paths, we both agreed on a management position in Wood Fiber Supply, or a supervisory and management position in either Pulp & Paper or Timber and Wood Products. This is a broad category, but he feels it's important not to be too narrow in a company this size. The part he felt was very important was the ability to relocate, which I marked "yes." It may mean anywhere in the country, but any move would be temporary. Art was very pleased with that. So many people will not leave an area and it limits their career choices. I'm sure someday I'll want to say no more moving, but not yet. I'm just getting started.

The PRIDE review went very well, I thought. Then we did a performance review. This is where we agree on how I've performed on the important parts of the job. There are about thirty different aspects of the job. Six months ago, we had agreed on the relative importance of each. Now, we went through each one again and rated whether I performed better than average, average, or less than average, or need so much help that termination may be the best answer. We came out pretty close on most points, while on some, we differed and each gave in on a few. The result was I got "above average" on about eighty percent, so I think it was fair.

I have another project that's very interesting. I'm going to begin work on an MBA, Masters of Business Administration. City College in Seattle has a branch office in Port Angeles. The college is designed for working people and the classes are held in the evening. I'll start off with one class to see how it fits into my schedule. To register, I had to submit a letter of recommendation from someone saying I had enough brains to do the work. I asked the Port Angeles mill manager to write the letter for me and, what he wrote was very nice. This has been such a good week, even the rain is beautiful!

3/21/82

The Commodore's Ball was a great success. Fifty-five people attended and the award presentations were fantastic.

Did you hear that Mt. St. Helens blew again? It happened at night. The radio said there were so many helicopters around the mountain this morning it looked like bees around a hive.

My boss will be here for three days this week, so I'll be very busy. He likes to have a tight itinerary, including working breakfasts and dinners. After that, I have to drive to Portland for a seminar he's hosting. My boss is very people oriented and is constantly thinking of ways to upgrade our knowledge and improve our morale, so our whole department, including spouses, will attend a course called "Achieving Your Potential", a self-help psychology seminar.

4/4/82

Rain, rain, go away! When will it ever stop? We decided this weekend to act like summer was here anyway. We enjoyed a cookout Friday night with the foresters next door. Dinner included steamed clams, oysters in the shell cooked over an open fire, shrimp cocktail, salad, and desert. What fun! Today we had a picnic in the rain at a local park roasting hot dogs. I was amazed how many people were at the same park doing the same thing. I guess we all get a little stir-crazy here this time of year.

Last weekend was our whole department seminar in Portland including spouses. It was just great! There were thirty-six of us, husband and wives. Classes started Friday at 4 p.m. until 7, followed by a group dinner. In the lounge, we danced until 1 a.m.! Back in class Saturday 9-4 and Sunday 9-2. The classes consisted of 10 half-hour tapes followed by the major points reiterated by a husband/wife team, followed by ten minutes of workbook time per tape.

I was extremely pleased about Reinhard's reaction, which was very positive. It was like a light bulb turned on in his mind to even consider goals, such as motivating some of our yacht club members to get more involved and get the board of directors to work as a team.

"Achieving Your Potential" pulled together our mental thought processes, why we are the way we are, and how we can change our perception of reality in order to achieve what we really want in life. They started off by explaining that our conscious mind perceives the world through our sensory input. The subconscious mind records and stores our interpretation of reality and how we feel about our experience.

The creative subconscious maintains reality by making us act like the person we see ourselves to be. If we think we are not good at public speaking, when we have to make a speech, we blow it no matter what. It also provides the drive and energy to resolve conflict or accomplish a task. If we find ourselves in an uncomfortable situation, the subconscious mind gives us the energy to get back to where we belong.

I found it interesting that the subconscious does not know the difference between an actual experience and one we vividly imagine. That's why an event doesn't need to happen often for us to record a positive or negative attitude toward something. We just need to relive it often in our minds. To the degree that we vividly imagine an experience and feel it is happening in our imagination, it's stored in our subconscious as reality. So, if we want to make changes to our image of ourselves, we can use positive imagination to create a new picture of ourselves.

Lou Tice, the person who developed this program, gave an example of a small child who is told by his brothers or sisters that he can't draw and can't stay in the lines when he colors, and that his pictures are dumb. If told this often enough he will begin to believe it. Then he goes to school and the teacher asks him to draw and he thinks, "Like hell I will!" He challenged us to recognize where and how we habitually say negative or irrational things to ourselves, about ourselves, and change those into positive statements. Negative statements are inhibitive and keep us from doing the things we may want to do.

If we're uncomfortable with our current self-image, we can be motivated to act, but most of the time we try to change out of fear and pressure. This is saying to ourselves, "I have to…" and we end up blaming someone or something because we never accomplished what we said we had to do.

He said lasting motivation is based on saying "I want to…" or "I like to…" or "I feel good when I do…" When we use words like this, we accept responsibility for ourselves and our actions. For example, we see a dress we want. We see the dress, actually feel what it would be like wearing the dress, think how happy we would be to wear it, and by gosh, sooner or later we find a way to buy it. You can picture yourself doing something that when you get it, it feels like it was meant just for you. It fits like a glove.

Lou laid out these steps to make things happen for us. He said the key is to raise our self-image and the level of what we expect or want, and then our subconscious will give us the drive and energy to make those goals a reality. If we still tell ourselves that things are "too good for us" or that we would feel "out of place" doing something, we will subconsciously find ways to fail to achieve those things. We deliberately prepare ourselves for a pre-determined outcome.

He said after we have selected the things we want, whether personal or materialistic, then we should:

   * imagine the end result in vivid specific detail,

   * clarify the desire (what needs to be done in terms of time, money, effort and risk),

   * analyze the possible temporary setbacks that may need to be overcome,

   * see ourselves in the first person actually experiencing the desired end result with all our senses and emotions,

   * repeat the experience over and over (twice a day for three to five weeks),

   * lockout all negative or conflicting opinions, such as "I can't do it" or "That's not like me".

And the result is as our self-image changes, we will begin to accomplish the changes we desire. Interesting, isn't it?

Nothing in the course was really new, but he put it together and made it easy to understand. When you think of it, we all know of times when we wanted something really bad and, basically, that's how we got it. It should be fun to work with.

In July, I'll experience what it is like to be a Department Head. Art asked me to sit in for him when he goes on vacation for two weeks. It's a real opportunity to 'sit at the helm' and I'm very excited about it. It's also the time of year when our suppliers take an annual vacation, and this year plans to be longer than usual with the continuing bad market conditions. There probably won't be a dull moment.

4/20/82

Last Thursday morning the Civil Air Patrol asked for help looking for a pilot that had taken off on Sunday from Kitsap County Airport in poor weather, almost hitting another plane, and never returned.

Reinhard volunteered to help and flew down to Kitsap, about an hour from here. The Patrol had it all organized and assigned a spotter to fly with him in the area from Sequim Bay to east of Port Townsend. It was a 9-mile by 10-mile grid. They made quarter mile-wide passes and it took 2 hours to complete one pass. They flew at 500' altitude at eighty knots for five hours and didn't find anything. The Patrol filled up his gas tanks, so he came home with more gas than he started with. The plane was found on Friday about four miles from the airport in a heavily wooded area. The pilot did not survive.

5/2/82

I'm anxious to get your letter about all of the changes at the base. I assumed there would be a lot of changes when Reagan started whacking away at the spending programs. I bet you were hoping Mr. Olevitch would be your boss until you retired. Now you have a lot of new people to learn how to get along with. I looked for a book on coping with change, but the closest one I could find is in this package. Change is really a good thing, because it's time to dust off our ways of doing things and take a good look to see if maybe there isn't a better way, or just a different way to do it.

Every time I get a new boss, he makes me do things a little different, even if I happen to like the way things were. I figure if a certain way of doing things makes him feel a little better about how I do my job, then why not change. It's next to impossible to change my boss to doing things my way, plus it is frustrating and time consuming.

When I get a new boss, it takes me a while to figure out how he operates. Things that weren't important to my previous boss are important to the new one. Things that I thought were previously trivial now seem to be of the utmost importance. Everyone's thinking process is different and their decision-making process is different, so they need to receive information in different ways.

The boss I have right now is no doubt the best one I have ever had. I dread the day he gets promoted. There are definitely not enough people in this company like him. It's inevitable though, since there is nothing as constant as change. But I've learned important things from every boss I've ever had, whether I personally liked him or not.

I glanced through the Dr. Brothers book and in Chapter 11 she talks about the Big Switch; that men will put aside all differences and team up to get something done while woman tend to be unable to escape their like or dislike for someone. We don't overcome our emotions very well in order to get the job done. I'm getting better at it, but some days I should know better than to open my mouth to some people. No matter whether I like the person or not, I have to work with them, cooperate with them, and get them to cooperate with me, or else I'll be the one without the job.

Hope your days are a little brighter after this lady-to-lady chat. I love you very, very much and want you to think nothing but good thoughts until we see you. A fellow once told me there were only four kinds of people in the world, so by now you should be pretty good about dealing with all of them.

6/6/82

Our third yacht club outing was last weekend and ended in a rescue mission. We were cruising slowly around Sequim Bay when a plane flying lower than usual went by us. We waved and the pilot dipped his wings in reply. Within two minutes, people on the dock started yelling at us and pointing down to the end of the bay. Then we heard on the CB that the plane had gone down after hitting a sailboat mast. We raced there as fast as we could and all we could see were small splinters and an oil slick. We marked the spot with our anchor right away.

It seemed like a minute later the volunteer firemen and a paramedic arrived. They were brought out to our boat, because it was the largest boat in the immediate area. Two local fellows, who skin dive for fun, also heard it on the CB and rounded up their gear and also came out to our boat. They dove down and pulled the pilot out of the plane and brought him aboard. The paramedic didn't waste a second and worked on him for forty minutes before the Coast Guard helicopter arrived and lowered a gurney. The firemen loaded the man on it and he was lifted into the helicopter and away they went.

I spent most of that time keeping other boats away from ours to keep it from getting dinged up. I also stowed gear up front and just stayed out of the way. Reinhard used our CB to talk to the local REACT team who communicated with the firemen and the helicopter. Later that day the wreck was pulled out of the water. Reinhard took a photo of the mangled plane and it ended up on the front page of the Daily News.

The ducks continue to surprise us and now we have three more babies. Cloudy hatched the eggs and they are cute. The two male adults were banished from the pen and have been roaming the yard. Their favorite spots to loaf around are in the carport  by the sliding door making piles of poop and sitting on the fence by the pond.

By the way Ginger is a he! We had a surprise party for one couple in the club who are getting married. We had oysters in the shell on our wood stove in the sun room and lots of goodies. One of the guests said Ginger was definitely not a she. I asked how he knew, and he picked up Ginger and said, grab here (you can imagine where!). What a shock to me! Now Reinhard calls him George, since I can't seem to find a male name that fits.

"He" has learned to use the doggy door downstairs so he can go in and out any time. It's convenient, but we do keep the door to the upstairs closed when we're gone. Now since he's outside so much, he won't use the litter box just when I'm getting free kitty litter. Crown Z is making litter out of paper mill sludge, which is wood particles that typically go out before the waste water goes back into the river. The litter was ready to go on the market when the company lawyers stopped it. Apparently, some claims on the bag could be seen as false and open the company to potential lawsuits. The company has a warehouse full of it and it's too expensive to re-bag, so they're giving it away to employees. How something like that could ever happen, I don't know.

I'm working on three critical projects at the moment. One involves working with Hermann Brothers Logging in Port Angeles to experiment how best we could make use of stagnated stands of trees on the Olympic National Forest. The forest has 15,000 acres of what they call "doghair." It's land that was destroyed by intense forest fires at the turn of the century and the trees grew back so thick that, eight decades later, the trees only average 8" in diameter or less.

Throughout the years, not one acre was thinned, so today, instead of 300 trees per acre, typical of a managed forest in this area, there are 2,000 to 40,000 trees per acre. You can see by the photo how thick the forest is. You can't even walk through it.

We have been lobbying the Forest Service to let us cut 700 acres a year of these stagnated stands of trees. After a few months of meetings with both the Hermann Brothers and the Olympic National Forest Supervisor's team, an experimental thinning was approved to find out if the trees left behind were thinned would they start to grow? Thanks to Bill and Steve Hermann who invested in the equipment to thin the trees, load them on a log truck, and take them to Crown's Chimacum Log Yard. A portable chipper was set up in the log yard. The trees were chipped, blown into a van, and hauled to Port Townsend. The chips were put onto a special pile, since the bark on the trees was mixed in with the wood chips.

Here is the edge of the thinning operation. Amazing difference! I don't remember how large an area was thinned, but we had to laugh as the Hermann Brothers crew wrangled the doghair to get it to stay on a regular log truck. What a mess! Debris fell alongside the road from the landing to the log yard.

With the new chippers on the market, it's now possible to run this small diameter material through a whole log chipper and make quality chips for our Port Townsend paper mill. The tree tops are processed through a portable hammer hog and used in our boiler to make electricity.

At one point, the brothers felt that some of the trees were large enough that a section of the trees could be made into 4"x4" cants, which would be a higher value product. The next piece of equipment they brought in was a portable sawmill to cut 6-8' logs into cants that could be sold and then sawn into 2"x4" lumber.

We felt that the larger project would be a good deal for the Forest Service, because they would get the land cleared and replant it with a new forest. The stumbling block is money. With all of the government cutbacks, there aren't funds available at the moment for the Forest Service to lay out a harvest plan for these acres. My next step is to put together a presentation covering the benefits to a program like this and present it to the Forest Service at the local, regional, and federal level. It may entail a trip to Washington, DC to visit Max Peterson, the Chief of the Forest Service.

I spent quite a busy week on the road. Did I tell you I've turned over 80,000 miles on my car? I felt really tired that day just knowing I drove all of those miles. This week I go to Portland for two days, then back home, then back to Portland for two weeks to sit in for my boss. There are incredible supply problems for our Columbia River mills in that area and I've heard that the Portland office is a real zoo. At the same time, I'm getting our wood fiber inventories down real low, so Mac will have to watch everything very closely while I am gone.

This Tuesday, I will give my first presentation to the Forest Service in Olympia on the doghair proposal. I have a slide show and a booklet prepared. It will be interesting to get their reaction. Then, in a couple weeks, I'll present it to the Regional Forester in Portland, who manages nine national forests.

Yesterday, we had fun with the Royal Dungeness Yacht Club, a loosely organized group of people who live about five miles north of Sequim on the straits. They are our age, but they're all sail boaters. They had their annual sailboat race on Sequim Bay and invited us to go along on one of the sailboats. It was a great race…just my style…no wind! A half-hour race took an hour and a half. The committee boat was a powerboat that cruised from boat to boat to make sure no one was cheating, but their most important job was refilling beer mugs! The committee boat had a 16-gallon keg on board and afterwards, there was a beach party to finish off the keg. A nice way to end a hectic week.

Today I spent most of the morning working on my term paper for the master's program. It is a good thing I'm only taking one class or I would never be able to fit all of the work in.

I decided we should have a "Roll Your Own Eggroll Party" at the clubhouse on Father's Day to coincide with a sailboat and dingy race. I found the wrappers in the grocery and will make the fillings.

6/18/82

We're having record temperatures this week and right now it is 86 degrees. It's quite something for June, since it's typically our wettest month. It always rains during the Irrigation Festival. Last year it rained 21 days in June and this year nothing. The result is that Reinhard is flying fire patrol 7 days a week. I took a half day vacation just so I could enjoy this weather. It doesn't take long to get a sunburn since we're so white. It's called Washington White…not that it rains a lot out here, it's just that sunny days usually occur during the week.

This week I met with the Forest Service regional management team in Portland about the doghair project and some of it ended up in an article in *Timber West Magazine* (see the appendix). It turned out pretty good.

6/27/82

It's finally raining after a month of no rain, a welcomed relief to the farmers. Even our irrigation ditch is dry so we're using our thousand-gallon storage tank for water.

Our baby ducks are growing up so fast. Cloudy, the adult female, is now sitting on 15 more eggs. We're going to have to make some decisions here pretty soon. How many ducks are enough? Ginger is very jealous of the ducks. When we feed the fish, the ducks come running, and so does the cat. Ginger pushes the ducks away, even though he won't eat their food. He doesn't want us feeding those ducks!

The egg roll party was a huge success. We made 120 egg rolls and there wasn't one left. We had three types: shrimp and ham, hamburger and mushrooms, and turkey with veggies.

More changes at work and I expect this will continue most of the year unless the market for lumber and paper improves. Remember the Timber VP who refused to get along with the Pulp & Paper VP and their problems were pushed up to the Exec level where they still couldn't be ironed out? Last week an announcement was made that the Pulp & Paper VP is also taking over the Timber Department. It's a hard lesson to learn. In this company, Pulp & Paper is king and if you push your luck on the timber side, you're going to lose.

It was a real shock for most of the timber people, especially in Portland. They were walking the halls in disbelief. I was the first to break the news to Diane. We were having lunch about an hour after the announcement. She just sank in her chair. The problem is she's so loyal to her boss, the Timber VP, she has not made many friends in the company. The other chip buyers tell me that it means over time her boss will be pushed out of the company and she will be out on a limb. That's the dangerous thing about hooking onto someone else's star—if they fall, so do you. Anyway, I do feel for her. My boss says this is just one many changes to come.

7/12/82

Here I am again in Portland for my second week as "the boss." I flew down this morning and went to a meeting at our Central Research Division near Camas. I think I could get use to this! Art's office is a larger corner one on the fifth floor. Such a difference from the decade's old offices at the mills.

7/26/82

Except for weekends, I was in the Portland office from June 30 to July 17. It was a great experience. Everyone in the department was really super about it. One fellow is a bit resentful, but he used to be our department head and is the one who hired me, so I understand. Nothing monumental or earth shattering happened during that time, but a few problems came up that we solved as a group. I did contribute to building our relationship with the Timber group that disowned us since they were recently put under the Pulp & Paper label. I invited myself to their staff meetings and met with their controller and operations manager on the side.

Settsu Linerboard Company, a Japanese linerboard corporation, is interested in going into a joint venture at Port Townsend. Crown is very interested in selling half of the plant just to get some capital to invest in the old mill. Our company cannot afford to put money into it since we have so many other old mills that need modernization. I spent two days and two evenings with ten Japanese (only two could speak English), Bill Gionatti from our headquarters who is heading up the venture, and the PT mill manager and assistant manager.

On Tuesday, I took a group of Japanese to the woods to see our chipping operations. I called Pat at the Waddycallit Deli and told her I needed a tailgate lunch. She said the Japanese eat light lunches so she would fix some crepes and insisted we must have Henry Weinhard's beer. She said the Japanese love Henry's. Crepes and beer? I was hesitant to say okay, but am I glad she insisted.

It was a misty rainy day, so the first thing I had to do was outfit them in rain gear from the mill. Next, we went to see the Crown chipper operating in the Chimacum log yard, then picked up lunch and headed for the woods. The lunch trays were filled with quartered deli sandwiches and crepes along with a cold case of Henry Weinhard's beer. The crepes were salmon and crème cheese, roast beef and crème cheese, turkey and herb butter. They were delicious and very easy to eat, just like a roll.

Mr. Suzuki, the CEO of Settsu, said he had been in the U.S. for a week and this was the best lunch so far. I had to initially show them how to eat all of this from the tailgate, but they caught on fast. We were standing in the mist surrounded by trees, eating crepes and drinking beer, and just like a little boy Mr. Moragami exclaimed, "This is just like camping!" I cracked up! The tour in the woods was a real success.

The next day I was in an all-day meeting with the group explaining our fiber supply situation. Rick from our Portland office came up and covered the west coast supply and demand balance and I handled the Puget Sound balance. It was a very long day. Everything we said had to be repeated by an interpreter for the Settsu team, and there were many questions.

On Thursday evening, the mill management hosted a dinner for Settsu in one of the officer's houses at Ft. Worden State and

Historical Park, near the mill and where a lot of the movie Officer and a Gentleman was filmed. I was the only woman and it was fascinating for the Japanese. They asked me things like "Mary-san, who is cooking dinner for your husband tonight?" to which I replied, "If he's hungry, he will fix it himself." They laughed and laughed. "When you interviewed for a job with Crown Z weren't they afraid to hire a woman?" I explained equal opportunity and the push to get more women into management positions. I could tell they had a hard time imagining it.

Dinner began with raw salmon, raw red snapper, marinated crab, grapes and olives, and steamed mussels. I ate the mussels and crab and took one bite of each raw fish and left the rest. Thank goodness the rest of the dinner was American filet mignon.

After dinner, things perked up when Mr. Suzuki (#1 man) stood up and burst into song. I was thinking you've got to be kidding me! Then he sang an American love song in English, even though he doesn't speak it. Another Japanese stood up and sang Moon River, then another and another. Naturally I was concerned about the rotation getting around to me. Our Crown Z Asia pulp salesman, who is also Japanese, was also at the dinner. He also sang, but he had a few drinks too many and sang a song in Japanese about geisha girls using hand expressions. It was hilarious! Everyone was doubled over with laughter including myself. One of the other Japanese said "Ok Mary-san I don't think we should interpret that." And I said "No interpretation needed, I understand," and everyone laughed even harder.

Then the Crown Z rep said they should hear from a soprano voice. Bill leaned over and said I didn't have to sing, but I cleared my throat and said I was from Irish decent and wanted to sing an Irish song. Then I stood up and sang "When Irish Eyes are Smiling." All the while I kept wondering if I would remember all of the words.

In the back of my mind, I could hear Uncle Bud really singing up a storm at our family gatherings and I finished the song just as he did. There was a lot of applause, but then I had to answer questions…no, I wasn't born in Ireland…no, my parents weren't born in Ireland. They must have wondered why I mentioned it at all.

Anyway, Mr. Suzuki was impressed enough to invite me to a dinner they were giving the next night for the pulp mill management team. In fact, the assistant manager tracked me down Friday afternoon out in Forks just to be sure I would be there and not disappoint them. Dinner that night was much quieter…maybe they all had hangovers. Dinner was prime rib and afterwards only Mr. Suzuki sang. The song was in Japanese about friendship. He also did a magic trick! Believe it or not the CEO knows magic. He cleared the table and borrowed two coins and somehow made both coins end up in one hand. He did it three times. The four of us from the mill received nice gifts: calculators, coasters, scissors, and paper dolls. As I was saying goodbye many of them said, "Tell your husband thank you!" It was a very wonderful experience, but very draining.

8/25/82

I'm almost finished with my class on Business Law for this quarter. It's more work than usual since my term paper is thirty-five pages long. Other people in the class say this is the hardest class so far, but I really liked it.

Our company has offered early retirement to people over fifty-five. They will pay a bonus until they reach sixty-five so they end up getting full benefits. Mac, who works for me, is going to take it. He said he would be working for nothing if he didn't. It means I will get a new assistant. The end result of early retirement is to get rid of bodies so the replacement will also have to pick up other duties from the mills and overall, there are fewer hours worked. I'll have to spend a lot of time around the PA mill when the replacement starts to keep an eye on things, so I may not be able to take another class for a while.

We have 11 new baby ducks in the big pen by the pond. My how they proliferate! Now they have plenty of room to play with running water. They sure eat a lot and are so cute.

9/7/82

Summer is officially over and it sure was a short one. Reinhard only flew half the number of hours he did last year. The news said it was a record year for the smallest number of forest fires.

This was the first weekend in almost three months that I didn't have to study or do something for work. What a thrill! We washed windows instead. It was fun. I also started a new book "Anna

Karenina" by Leo Tolstoy, which is fairly interesting. It feels so good to just do what I feel like doing for a change.

As you can probably tell, this typewriter is not working so well these days. It wants to go ½-1 line on return instead of two. It was very frustrating when I was typing my term paper.

Remember I told you Mac, my assistant, is retiring? He will be replaced and I glad about that. Some management people wanted to see the job split between someone at Port Townsend and someone at Port Angeles. My boss, Art, asked me to put together my reasons why I believed it was not a good idea and to make a recommendation. My thinking turned out to be an 8-page analysis of three options. Art was very pleased with the analysis and heartily accepted my recommendation not to split the job.

Art has a new boss also, so it took quite a bit of explaining to that person what we wanted to do and why. The tentative replacement for Mac is a woman who works in the Port Angeles Technical Department, Glenda, who is really on the ball. I'm very pleased and looking forward to working with her. She will start next week and get two weeks training by Mac. By the time he leaves, she will be at that thoroughly confused stage, so I'll have to make extra time to stay on top of things for a while.

10/2/82

Last weekend, the forester's ducks ended up as their original names forecasted, Christmas and Thanksgiving. It was getting to be too much. Too much manure on their patio. We aren't through with ducks though. Cloudy just hatched 11 ducklings. We have them in the shed and yes, again, they are so cute!

10/30/82

Last night was the grand opening of our sauna, between our house and the foresters, Steve and Don. Together we built it out of cedar from Butcher's Pole Yard, turned an old water tank on its side and turned it into a wood stove, put in benches, and it sits eight. We have an extension telephone in it and Steve put in speakers under the seats hooked up to his stereo in the house. This morning, I tried to make oatmeal cookies to celebrate the sauna, but what a disaster. I reread the recipe and noticed that I forgot flour. Yep, we must have had a good time last night.

We went to the Hood Canal Bridge opening last weekend. All of the politicians were there and every one of them wanted to make a speech. About half of the audience was media. The picture is the bridge now ready to be used again. What a pleasure it is now to only use one ferry to go to Seattle.

It was announced yesterday that our Canadian operations are being sold to a New Zealand corporation. What? No one in the field saw this coming. I buy a lot of chips through Crown Canada, so this may change our relationship a lot.

11/15/82

This past weekend we went to Seattle on Friday afternoon for a tugboat dedication at Foss. It was their new tractor tug, a 4000 hp beauty that can go in any direction. It took off from the dock sideways, turned on a dime, and went as fast backwards as forwards and stopped in its own length.

There were the typical cocktails and goodies and then a beautiful christening ceremony. The president's wife broke the champagne bottle on the bow at that same instant a fire boat nearby put up an 8-spray salute, and all of the tugs and boats in the area blasted their horns. It was delightful!

12/5/82

I was notified Sunday afternoon that there were two meetings I needed to be at the <u>next day</u> in Portland. While I was there, I had my annual performance appraisal. This is done using a list of about 30 qualities that are graded separately by both the boss and subordinate as to whether the subordinate's performance was excellent, very good, good or poor during the year. Then the boss and subordinate compare their ratings and iron out the differences. Next, both sign the agreement that includes how to improve any deficiencies. I had no deficiencies, so mine came out so good I was surprised and impressed, too, that my work has been recognized.

My salary review is in April, but Art put in for a merit raise early and it was approved. He said it was the first time he ever did that, but he said I deserved it. I was walking on clouds the rest of the week.

1983

1/27/83

Last weekend we splurged and bought a Commander Vic 20 home computer. It was on sale for $179 and we couldn't resist. It's amazing how many things it can do: music, graphics, change colors, and the programming is easier than I ever imagined. Now the evenings are filled with computing and it is a nice change from watching TV.

Enclosed are a couple articles from a timber magazine you might find interesting. One of them is on the doghair project I have been working on for so long. We are making progress, but it's very slow. (See the appendix.)

Reinhard's term as commodore of the yacht club is coming to an end. Most of the membership wants him to continue, but he is ready to just enjoy the club again instead of continually pushing to get things done. This year will be a very important one for the club since the marina will start to be built this summer and the club will need to find a new building. The clubhouse is scheduled to become the parking lot so we need to either have fundraisers to buy property or hope the port donates a site for us and then foot the bill for a building.

It's been ten years since John Wayne donated the twenty-two acres of land along Sequim Bay for a marina and paid over a million dollars for an Environmental Impact Review to bring the marina into reality. The story goes that Wayne came to Sequim Bay frequently on his yacht "Wild Goose" and fell in love with it. The new facilities will include moorage, marine services, a restaurant, showers, laundry and banquet facilities, and provide boat launch ramps, fuel facilities, public beach access and picnic areas. It will be a great addition to the whole area.

Now back to me....

My how fast things change in the marketplace. All of a sudden lumber prices have soared the past month and sawmills can't produce enough lumber. Most are sure it won't last because the high level of demand initially just fills the pipeline. As soon as retailers have a full inventory, the orders will slow down. The big question is whether sales will slow down at the retail level for builders and homeowners.

At the same time the pulp market is in the pits. We have one machine curtailed at each mill. I had to curtail our chip supplier's fifty percent at a time when they want to make all of the lumber they can. If they can't get rid of their chips, they either stockpile them somewhere or have to stop producing lumber. It's a tough spot.

I even had a vice president of one supplier come to Port Townsend to see for himself if our mill was really curtailed. He said it's costing his company $50,000 a month in profit because they can't get rid of the chips. If we can't afford to make paper, there isn't much I can do about that. This is another part of the crazy cycles that I haven't experienced.

3/13/83

I haven't written lately because I had this term paper hanging over my head. Last weekend I spent the whole weekend finishing it up. On Sunday, I typed for six hours! The paper was twenty-seven pages. It was a marketing survey I did for the local weekly newspaper here in Sequim, The Jimmy Come Lately Gazette, A couple of months ago, a friend told me that the paper was not doing well, so I talked to the owner and offered to take a survey of the community. The results are in and I think she will get a lot out of the report.

Another potential buyer was at Port Townsend last week. I spent two days with them explaining fiber supply. I don't think they're going to buy it because it's going to take too much money to update the mill so it's profitable. It's still a mill built in 1928 that is still making low value products. I hear another company is expressing some interest, so I'll go through our story again in a few weeks.

I had a long talk with Art about the potential sale of the Port Townsend mill. He wants some continuity up here and hates to put a new buyer in right now. In order to keep me growing and learning, he asked me to find an area of the company I wanted to learn more about or maybe a seminar I want to go to and he would make the time available to do it. I have decided I want to learn more about running a tree farm and buying logs. I have talked to Frank, the new tree farm manager, and we have put a plan together that, for a few hours a month, I'll be learning something new and broadening my experience.

3/27/83

Last Thursday I was out in the woods for a day with Crown's timber cruiser, Terry Gilmore. I learned timber cruising in college, but wanted to learn The Crown Z grading scale for the quality of the trees coming off the tree farm. I was pretty sore and tired in the evening because of the steep hills we climbed all day. We saw some tree damage that wasn't typical of what I had seen earlier—the bark was hanging lose in strips. Terry said it was bear damage. Ah, I knew I wasn't cut out for timber cruising!

6/8/83

Note: Although Mother and I talked a couple of times a week, there is a large gap in letters about work and it's because of a signed letter of intent to sell the Port Townsend mill to Haindl Paper Ltd., a West German paper company. Haindl is the largest manufacturer of newsprint in the European Community.

The new company---a U.S. subsidiary of Haindl—would be created to oversee PT mill operations. Juan del Valle would become president of that company and representatives of the parent company would serve on the board of directors.

Haindl is a family-owned company founded in 1849. Its board chairman is Ernst Haindl. The company produces newsprint, glossy magazine paper, wood-containing coated roll papers, and other print and writing papers. Port Townsend would be the firm's first manufacturing venture outside of West Germany.

Del Valle, 50, the man who helped negotiate the sale, was born in Panama, and was employed as a pulp mill foreman for Weyerhaeuser. He later ran several Boise Cascade mills and became executive vice president in charge of pulp and paper products for the company before he joined Haindl.

Haindl began negotiating with Crown for the purchase of the mill over a year ago. Why this particular mill? "Location mainly," del Valle responded. "I think the export market is going to expand and this is a good mill to export from. It's not a good location to service the United States, but it's good for outgoing freight. You can ship to Japan cheaper than to San Francisco.

In a separate article, the Association of Western Pulp and Paper Workers Local 175 was pleased by reports that Haindl plans to invest more than $100 million to modernize the facility and increase production.

6/16/83

The morning after arriving home from vacation, I had a 9 a.m. meeting at Port Townsend with the purchasing agent, the mill manager, and assistant manager. We were told of the sale of the mill and were given a position statement to pass on to suppliers. At that same hour in San Francisco, the corporate spokesperson broke the news to the media. At 9:30 the manager announced it to the union and the assistant manager read the prepared statement to the salaried people.

It wasn't a surprise the mill was sold, but it was a surprise that all of the people at the mill would be officially terminated by Crown and have to interview to be rehired by Haindl. That doesn't affect me since I work for Portland, but it really bothers the employees, but Haindl insisted it be part of the deal. This gives them a clean break to make changes in personnel and the union contract.

Right now, the mill is an unbleached kraft mill that makes grocery bags, linerboard, and other brown paper grades, as well as unbleached pulp. Haindl plans to put in a bleached plant, plus add production capacity, and boost the production from 430 tons of paper a day to 600 tons per day over a two-year period. The main product would then be bleached kraft pulp. The effect on the chip supply will be to add 150,000 units to the mill demand. That is about 12,000+ per month or 20 barges or 1200 truckloads of additional chips each month. I might need some help to make that happen, that is if I get to keep my job with the new company.

Last Thursday, I was asked to meet the person who will be the new company president, Juan del Valle. He was #2 at Boise Cascade in pulp and paper at one time. He really knows the business. I picked him up at the Winslow ferry terminal and we had breakfast. I had barely sat down and the questions started coming. He asked real in-depth questions and what I consider the right ones about fiber supply. There was another company looking at Port Townsend that I talked with that started off with the question "What is a chip?"!!!

It was very obvious that Juan knew the chip business. He's close friends with the presidents of some of my supplying companies. We got along well and at the end of two hours of questions, he asked me to come with the new company. I told him I would definitely consider it, but I knew my boss was looking for something for me in Crown Z and I would have to consider both options. He said fine, but as soon as I make up my mind to let him know. He hopes it's soon, because if I don't go with him, he'll have to hire someone who is already experienced in the business away from another company. That takes time, so he needs as much time as he can get.

Haindl takes over officially October 1st. Juan can't afford to take the time to train someone in the wood fiber supply job. Because it takes so long, I do have a definite advantage. When I told Art, he said definitely no, he wants me to stay with Crown. He said he would talk to Bill Corbin, Exec VP of Timber and Wood Products about a position. A couple days later, he asked me if we would mind moving…to Mississippi. I said I would consider any opportunity, but for Mississippi I would like to go down and see the area and the job first. He said no problem, but I haven't heard anything further.

Apparently, the Timber Department just got approval to build a brand-new state-of-the-art sawmill in McComb, Mississippi and I could be part of the building and startup, which would be a great experience. Reinhard said he would go wherever the opportunities were, but Ginger wanted to stay in the Northwest! I wondered why?

Yesterday I had to go to Seattle to meet with Juan again, but this time Doug (PT mill manager) was there also. He wanted us to meet one of the German owners, who noticed right away that my last name (Schroeder) was German. He asked me about the same questions and how I would find the extra wood for the expansion when they needed it in two years at the flick of a switch, without increasing the inventory or raising the price.

The discussion went well, but it was a bit odd with Doug there. He and I don't see eye-to-eye all of the time. He has been known to pull the rug out from under me in the best of company, so I'm always on guard when he's around. In general, things went well. This Sunday I meet Juan again in a general Q&A session with other salaried people at the mill. It will be held at the Port Ludlow resort. Apparently, it will be a beer and pretzel session with open questions and answers.

Juan will be setting up the headquarters office in Winslow, on Bainbridge Island. That is where the ferry docks when we come home from Seattle and it's a beautiful area. He wants the office off site of the mill property and only have with him the financial expert, pulp salesman, and chip buyer. He will have a new mill manager to handle production. I imagine working for him will be tough, but what a learning experience. He knows the business very well, so standards will be very high. There might be opportunities for me to expand into other areas, since I assume he will be looking into other business ventures for Haindl.

If I take the job, we'd probably live in Poulsbo, about 11 miles from Winslow. It's a Scandinavian community, a bit like Leavenworth, with decorated store fronts in the downtown, which is right on the water, and has a very nice marina and boat launch.

After I get back from Portland I will know more. I didn't expect to have to make this decision so soon after the announcement, but here we are hanging in midair. There doesn't seem to be enough other work I could do at the Port Angeles mill to fill out a 40-hour week. Sixty percent of my time is spent on Port Townsend. Even if there was fill-in work at PA, I imagine it wouldn't be very exciting. Make-work projects don't offer much of a challenge.

6/17/83

Intra-Company Memo from Art Stebbins, Fiber Supply Manager, to all facility managers:

Mary Schroeder is currently Fiber Procurement Supervisor for the Puget Sound area. With the sale of the Port Townsend mill, most of her workload will be eliminated and her position will also most likely be eliminated as the Port Angeles mill will not require a full-time Fiber Supply person.

The buyers of the PT mill have been favorably impressed with Mary and have offered her the fiber procurement responsibility for the mill, which would be a full-time job with the expansion they have planned. She would strongly prefer to stay with CZ, however, if we can provide employment which could lead toward her career objective of upper middle line management in the Pulp & Paper or Timber & Wood Products divisions.

Attached are copies of her most recent performance reviews and PRIDE sheets, and selected material from her personnel file. I have noticed exceptional growth in this employee in my time in this department and suspect exceptional growth potential. Her determination and general effectiveness are well above average. We should be looking for an appropriate position for her quickly as her prospective new employer would like a decision soon. She would be available for transfer between now and October.

7/2/83

I haven't heard anything yet on another position in Crown. My boss is looking hard for me. He said if nothing comes up before Haindl needs an answer that I could keep the work at the PA mill and do some special projects to fill in the day. That wouldn't be so bad.

It depends on the offer from Haindl. It would be risky to go with the new company, because I don't know enough about them and until they own the mill we really don't know for sure what their plans are. They say they are going to do certain things, but they're under no obligation to do them. I heard the other day that Crown wants to sell the tree farm up here and that it is officially for sale. Bit by bit, Crown Z is moving toward the objective of concentrating only on the Columbia River/Portland area and in the south.

Crown Z timberland

8/7/83

Two weeks ago, I took Juan del Valle around to meet our chip suppliers. I was with him from noon Tuesday until 2 p.m. Friday. I had to arrange car rentals, airline tickets, and hotel arrangements. It was a whirlwind tour from Seattle to Vancouver, Canada to Victoria and back to Port Angeles. Breakfasts, lunches, and dinners were full of meetings. It was long enough that you really get to know a person. I know now that there is no way I would work for him. He seems to think it's cute to have a woman chip buyer, but I think he really feels it doesn't make good business sense. I'm glad that decision is made, and now I can look forward to a new position with Crown.

Last Tuesday I interviewed for a job at Headquarters in San Francisco, to be Financial Manager of the Logistics Department (Transportation). 45% of the job is cost savings projects, which would be very interesting since it would expose me to all of the pulp and paper business operations and customers. With all of the transportation deregulation going on, there are a lot of opportunities to save money in freight. I will know next week if I am one of the finalists.

Another area of interest is Timber and Wood Products. Crown is going to build that sawmill in McComb, Mississippi and will have about six jobs open that I would qualify for. When I talked to the head personnel man in the south, he asked me if I would prefer to work for Northwest Timber. I told him the whole division is in such

be a very good place to get into right now. The VP of NW Timber is quite a tyrant resulting in several resignations, which upset San Francisco quite a bit.

The personnel manager shared with me that Crown can't put up with the problems in Northwest Timber much longer, because it is damaging the company and that the problem would be solved very soon. This past Tuesday the VP of Timber in Portland was fired! You can't imagine how excited all of the timber people are, as well as me. Now I would be thrilled to get into Timber here.

This past week my boss, Art, came up for two days to visit the mill managers and see what's happening. He was thrilled about the change in Timber and is determined to help me find the right job. He worked in the south for 8 years and loved it, so he keeps telling me how great it is and how I'll love it. Well, we'll see.

Last weekend we cruised to Fort Flagler near Port Townsend for the annual Timber picnic. They cooked salmon over an open alder fire and had buckets of oysters and clams. It was one of those perfect days, clear skies and no wind. I made coleslaw with my precious Marzetti dressing (I have to parcel it out so I have enough until you can send more.) On Sunday it was so windy on the Strait, we couldn't make it back, so we called our neighbors and they drove over to get us.

8/30/83

Wow, are things moving fast! The job in San Francisco is mine and it needs to be filled right away. The Port Angeles mill is having a cocktail party for me tomorrow night at one of the local restaurants. All of the salaried people at the mill are invited to say a few words. Usually, the comments are funny things, like a roast. I'm working on a few lines myself, so I'll get back at some of them. It should be fun.

This week Don Hansen, my old boss, is here trying to learn all that is happening so he can take my place at Port Angeles starting next week. Some of the people up here aren't too happy about it, because they remember when he was my boss. Unfortunately, Don doesn't come across very well, even though he is a hard worker and knows the business. The arrangement is that he will be here until the Port Townsend mill is sold to Haindl. At that time, he is scheduled to go back to the Portland office. He has other ideas and hopes to make my job at PA into a full-time job and move up here. It isn't a full-time job, but if they add some duties to it, it could be. I will be surprised if he can pull that off.

My new job in San Francisco is so exciting because I will be doing project work on the new Wood Products Group strategy. They want to put enough money into the two sawmills we are operating to make them saleable. One is just south of Portland in Estacada and the other is in Omak, Washington.

Crown is working on approval to build a new high-tech sawmill near Astoria, Oregon on the coast, then buy and modernize a nearby sawmill called Dant & Russell. The Logistics Dept. in San Francisco doesn't have many people with knowledge about sawmill management, finance, etc. so they are very happy that I'm coming on board. They are all overworked and are glad to have the help.

Together we're labeled as a Task Force assigned to pull all of this off. The head person is Jim Quinn, previously mill manager at the Omak sawmill. In addition, there are four guys who also worked at the Omak mill. I can see they don't have a wide range of experience putting together package deals like this. Their next presentation is in October and it will be their third one. Their previous presentations were on why the company ought to spend $50 million on this strategy without doing any market studies on where they would sell the products! Hard to believe, but they did. Now they aren't sure what information they need or what to present and want me to jump on that aspect of it and get it done before October.

As I get settled in San Francisco next week I'll give you a call. They said they already have a desk and telephone for me and I will have a beautiful view of Market Street, but then again this is a photo of Market Street, the main drag in downtown.

9/29/83

Sorry it's been so long since my last letter, but you can guess how busy we've been. Things changed and this new position will not be in San Francisco, but will be in Portland for a few months. This is my third week working in the Portland office and the third week in a motel room at the Marriott next door.

That reminds me, last Friday, the Wood Fiber Supply Dept. had a luncheon for me at Sweet Tibbie Dunbars here in Portland. There were nine of us. The waiter was so bad it was hilarious. The restaurant is very fancy, which made it even funnier. He took all of the drink orders and brought mostly wrong drinks and set each one down at the wrong spot. We said that wasn't ours and he just picked it up and sat it in front of the next person, who said it wasn't theirs either.

As this merry-go-round went on, he got really nervous. Then he took the lunch orders and, lo and behold, it happened again. We were really cracking up by this time. He would pick up the plate and set it in front of the next person who would say it wasn't theirs either! Marilyn, our secretary, was eating a salad and while she was eating, she had her fork held up with her elbow on the table. All of a sudden, the waiter grabbed the fork right out of her hand! One of the fellows asked why he did that and he said he would bring her another one. Apparently, he thought she didn't want that one. Then came dessert and, amazing, it happened again. By this time, it was so funny tears were running everywhere. Finally, the waiter said he must be having a nightmare and all of us were in it.

During dessert it was time for the group to roast me, but most of the comments were awfully nice. Then I got to talk about them. I told them when people ask me what so and so is like to work with in Fiber Supply, I related each of them with a TV or movie personality. Then I went around the table and described each person with a popular personality. They all seemed to enjoy it. Then I pulled out color copies of a "Thank You" drawing and each one of them is on it. One of our team, Lamar, is a good cartoonist and he did the drawings of each person complete with their TV or movie personality. Everyone loved it.

10/31/83

It has been quite a while since I wrote, but you can imagine how crazy things have been. I lose track of the days and where I should be when. Our new address is Rt. 1, Box 901A, Suquamish, WA 98392. We just rented a nice 3-bedroom home on a hill with a great view of the Columbia River.

Two weeks ago on Wednesday, I came back to Sequim to start pitching things out and cleaning. We worked on the house, garage and yard for five days, all the while wondering when we were going to move.

The confusion started on Tuesday. Juan called me at the Portland office and asked how I liked my new job. He said he was getting ready to buy the mill and asked if I would be interested in going to work for him. I asked what the job would be and he said I would be doing all of the Fiber Supply work as before, plus head the Transportation Dept. I would be responsible for seeing all of the products made at the mill delivered to the customers. I would negotiate the transportation contracts for truck, barge, rail and ship movements. That got me real excited!

Right now, the mill produces 450,000 tons of paper a year. Juan plans to increase that to 650,000 within two years. If all of the 450,000 were loaded into trucks, it would be an additional 9,000 trucks/year, but it would be shipped many different ways. There are already two people in the PT Shipping Dept. who take care of getting the products loaded and on their way. The contract arrangements and agreements are done in Portland right now, so I'd also take over that part. And the best part, it would pay $50,000/year.

After that, Juan said I can help just run the whole thing. So, it seems he will have 4-5 people to help him run the whole works, and I would be one of those.

The next morning, I told my boss, Jim Quinn, what had happened. He said it did sound like a good offer and if I wanted to put all of our things in storage for a month or so and think about it, it would be okay. Then I talked to my previous boss, Art, and he went through the pros and cons with me.

When I called Juan back at the end of the week, I asked him many questions about benefits, etc. I would get a company car. I tentatively told him I would take the job. He said after they sign the formal papers to buy the mill, he will call and we can finalize things. He said he would pay our moving expense, so we went ahead and let the movers come and pack things up and put it in storage until everything is final.

Over the weekend we decided to get a jump on things and look for a place to live near Poulsbo on the Kitsap Peninsula. Lady luck was smiling on us and we rented the second house we looked at. We explained the situation and the owners were fine with it. The new house three-bedroom house with full basement where there is a rec room with wet bar. It has a view of Agate Pass, between the Kitsap Peninsula and Bainbridge Island. It's great to watch the boats go through and at night we can see some of the lights in Seattle. Our new town has two taverns: The Tides Inn and The Tides Out.

On Thursday, I went back to Portland to work and Reinhard went to the new house. In the meantime, we called the people whose house we rented in Suquamish and explained everything. They were very understanding and we agreed to pay two weeks rent to cover this period.

Back in Portland for the week. I talked to Art again and Jim Quinn and both feel the Haindl offer is a great opportunity. Art had lunch with Bill Corbin, the Timber Exec VP and shared what was going on with me. Bill said he was impressed with how I was handling this and if things don't work out at Haindl, there would be a job for me at Crown anytime. Now I can't ask for more than that.

Isn't it the tough times that make us all appreciate the good times?

11/8/83

My Portland work has me at Crown's sawmill in Estacada for another week. I'm staying at the Red Fox Motel. The Safari Club is the only restaurant in town and is chock full of wild animal heads, including a whole polar bear on its hind legs. I've never seen so many in my life.

I'm here because my boss asked me to help establish some production reporting systems for the sawmill. It isn't too difficult, but no one here has been able to pull it all together. I don't understand why. This is an old growth (large log) sawmill that has lost money every month but one this year and they don't know why! It blew my mind! They've had a fast turnover of managers, which has something to do with it, but it's no excuse.

I'm making a lot of progress, but when you start with nothing, anything is an achievement. I am working with many people at the mill to find out what data they keep and then I'm putting it together to get daily production reports to see if what they are doing is better or worse than their plan numbers. How anyone can operate a mill without knowing where their problem areas are is appalling.

In talking with the people, they all suspected what was wrong, but couldn't put their finger on it. The guys running the mill are "good old boys" from the woods or have worked their way up in the mill and they have practically no financial management skills. My boss is tickled pink that I am getting to the bottom of things.

I gave Jim, my boss, a letter of resignation yesterday effective November 20. He knew it was coming since I told him about the offer when I received it. Today, he told me that if he had a sawmill manager's position open he'd give it me, but the new sawmill hasn't been approved yet.

11/28/83

As you can see by the spacing between lines, this typewriter is going haywire. It's just worn out. Well, leaving Crown Z wasn't as easy as I thought when the time came. They made me three offers during the last week; the last one was on the morning of my last day and was complete with a job description. The job at Port Townsend was solid, but I admired Crown's management to come up with a new offer in short order. My boss said not to hesitate to come back any time.

This week I found out my old boss, Art, had breakfast with Juan last week and told Juan that he could have me for a year or two, but that Crown wanted me back after that. I thought that was awfully nice of him.

My new job started and it's very hectic. Haindl has not purchased the mill yet, but that will occur on 12-21. Until then I'm negotiating new chip contracts with the suppliers to take effect 12-

21 and learning all about the new part of my job, transportation for all products out of the mill. Luckily, I have people under me who know what they're doing. They will take care of the day-to-day things and I will do contract negotiation, long range planning, and looking for alternative methods and opportunities to lower costs.

Today, I was told the railroad we use is going belly up. It's the Seattle-North Coast Railroad (SNC), which is a short hauler from Port Angeles to Port Townsend. SNC bought out the Milwaukee Railroad when it went bankrupt. It seems SNC hasn't been paying their bills and doing who knows what with the revenue and it finally caught up with them. We developed some alternatives this afternoon that are more expensive, but at least we're covered.

At the same time, the lumber market is not improving and some of our suppliers are curtailed, so chips are in short supply. When we take over the mill at the end of the month, we may find a zero inventory of some chip species. Juan had to laugh today when I told him all of this. He said it seems I walked into a hell of a mess and what did I think I was going to do about it? It'll be a challenge, that's for sure.

I went to see our new office in Winslow last weekend, which is a block from the ferry. Our office building is two-stories and we have the whole bottom floor. There are four corner offices that are quite large and I will have one of them. My Transportation Specialist, whom we haven't hired yet, will be in the office next to me. Here is the Winslow Ferry that takes us to Seattle.

12/12/83

My new job is going very well, but is a bit hectic with long hours. Taking over a company operation is quite involved. We don't officially take over until 12-21 so I am not able to do any purchasing yet. I'm putting together new long-term chip contracts with suppliers. Around the holidays it's a hassle, because if our lawyers aren't gone, our supplier's lawyers are, and time is flying by.

For the past three days we've interviewed people for the transportation position that will report to me. It's extremely tiring. The Employee Relations Manager and I did the interviewing. I'm really glad he was able to help. Some of these people sounded good on the phone and their resumes looked good, but after two minutes with them I was ready to say 'thank you for coming' and show them the door. Dick walked through the company benefits, etc. with each one so there was no preferential treatment of any one.

I can't wait for you to meet our executive secretary in the new office. Her name is Susie and she's from England. What a doll. She is 36, long blonde hair with a very quick wit. She keeps things light and cheerful, which is a welcome relief with the pressure everyone is under right now. She met her husband in England and he is from Bainbridge Island. He's 24 years old and going to college. She is top notch and we are all going to enjoy having her around.

12/27/83

The official purchase of the mill was the 21st and it is now owned by Haindl. Unfortunately, Haindl chose to shut down the mill and won't start up until January 2nd due to union negotiations. The cold weather has created a terrible mess at the mill since so many segments of the pulp and paper making process have not been shut down for decades, and pipes are busting everywhere. The salaried people at the mill are working long hours to keep it from becoming a disaster.

The interesting thing about a mill is that in every section of the mill if there is a problem, the flow of fiber can be diverted to the 'basement' and remixed, so the whole mill keeps operating no matter what. It runs 24-hours a day with no intended shut downs. With pipes and systems that have not been shut down for decades, right now things seem to be on the verge of collapse.

1984

1/15/84

I haven't written much because I've been putting in long hours and haven't had the energy. The chip end of the job is going okay, although there is a shortage of cedar chips and we're almost out. The mill had to switch to other grades of paper that don't require as much cedar. The trouble is those products aren't saleable right now and we're having to put them in inventory hoping to sell them soon. It's a heck of a way to start this new company.

Juan keeps asking how I will make it when he takes this out of my paycheck. I always come back with some comment like, "Yes, I'm trying to figure out how we're going to make it on food stamps." Then he laughs and it's okay.

I have figured him out a little bit. If he hassles me, I have to come right back at him and he backs off quickly. He knows I'm doing the best that can be done. I've even received a few pats on the back, so I figure everything's okay. He really hassles our pulp and paper sales manager, Dave. He rips Dave up almost every day, but Dave just kind of smiles and shrugs it off. I think if he would retaliate a bit, he'd be better off.

Our new Financial Officer, Paul, is another one who is very strong willed. He comes on in full battle gear. The first week he told me that I had to report to him each week on the volume of fiber I was buying. I looked at him and said, "Oh, really," and turned away. It took me a couple weeks to figure him out. If I let him intimidate me, it's even worse the next time, but if I go back at him immediately, he also backs off and can be a very nice person. He finally realized that I only report to Juan. Now we even spend time to chit chat and the people observing us can't seem to believe it.

The other part of my job, transportation, has taken a lot of work to set up since so much of it was done by Crown Z in Portland and San Francisco. I hired a Traffic Administrator who works with freight rates, estimates freight costs, and audits the freight bills. He's from Pendleton, Oregon, smart but quiet, and is doing a real good job. It's quite a step for him to leave a company that ships out five trucks a day to this one with over 20 trucks plus railcars a day.

The people loading the trucks, railcars, and barges frequently remind me that they've done their jobs for 15 years and "Crown has always done it this way." The fact that Crown is gone has not set in yet. It does get frustrating, but they are very patient with me, which I appreciate. It is different since I'm the boss, but they're also teaching me the ropes.

Our landlady told us she is putting the house we rent up for sale, so now we have to move again.

3/3/84

Today I had an argument with the chip sales manager, Debbie, at Pope & Talbot Sawmill, again over hog fuel. It's getting to be quite a problem. Their mill has more production than anyone around here can use. She's going to have to stockpile it somewhere real soon. Then the railroad called and said they were filing bankruptcy tomorrow. It wasn't one of my better days.

Note: We found a house to rent on the Kitsap Peninsula along Hood Canal about a mile south of the Hood Canal Bridge. It had 200' of waterfront and fantastic oyster beds along the shoreline. The living room and kitchen had perfect views of the Olympic Mountains. Heavenly!

4/1/84

We joined friends on their boat for a cruise up and down Hood Canal this weekend. We went south from Port Ludlow, under the bridge, and past our house, then past Bangor Submarine base where they dock the Trident subs. We were in the middle of the canal cruising about 8-10 knots.

In front of the base we saw four large power boats with Navy emblems that were loaded down with all kinds of gear, including radar, and they were spaced about ½ mile apart. They paced along with us as we cruised by and where one stopped another took over until we were out of their area. We knew one of the nuclear subs was in because we saw it come past our house a couple of days earlier. It was the USS Florida. We could see part of it as a silhouette against the hanger building. Just in case the captains had long-range listening devices aimed at us, we opened beers and toasted the subs and the base a few times.

Another Trident sub went by this afternoon and we captured it on video. There were two escort boats in front, one alongside and two in the rear. We heard on the news tonight that the Pacific Peacemaker, the nuclear protest sailboat, was heading up here from California this week.

I had lunch with Debbie from Pope & Talbot's this week to talk about the excessive amount of hog fuel their mill is continuing to put out. She is still pushing me to take more, but I had to stand firm. I've been able to get her to concede on price and pay some of the barge demurrage (a daily fee we pay if we don't unload the barge on time) and also they will haul 50% of their production to landfill. I could tell she was under a lot of pressure to stand firm. It's a pure supply and demand product and there is a lot more supply than demand right now.

I think I'm making headway with the transportation fellow that works for me. Apparently, he has never negotiated rate reductions with the railroads and he was being very stubborn about it. He told me reducing the rate was taking money out of the railroad's pocket. What about our pocket? Anyway, after much discussion about our jobs and how our goal is to have the most economic transportation costs for our company he gave it a try, and lo and behold it worked. Now he is on a roll and is going after rate reductions on six different rail lines and four truck hauls.

I told him my goal is to save the company $1.5 million this year on transportation. He looked at me like I was crazy, but now after our weekly talks he's beginning to see I really mean it. The nice thing about being new to this arena is that I can question everything.

Reinhard has been taking aerial photos of the 30,000 acre east end tree farm called the Puget Sound Tree Farm for Crown's Timber Division. Crown is determined to sell it this year. They wanted some aerial pictures for a brochure for potential buyers. When one of the foresters working on the sale took the photos to Portland, that idea was scrapped because they have already cut almost everything and what's left is 10-15-year-old stands that don't look so hot from the air. We had a good chuckle at that. We wonder what they thought it looked like after all of the overcutting they've done. So much for sustained yield.

Juan made an offer on that land last year. He had a consultant forester cruise it and estimated he should bid $19-28 million. Juan offered $24 million and Crown said they wanted $60 million. He told them they were crazy. The rumor right now is they would take $15 million, so I told Juan if he was still interested, he could probably get it for a song.

7/5/84

It's amazing how well the economy is bouncing back, although the increasing interest rates are still killing the housing and lumber market. The paper market is very good and lumber market very bad, so chip prices are going up since chips are getting hard to find.

I'm still working on our railroad problem. The Seattle-North Coast Railroad that carries our railcar tonnage officially went bankrupt two weeks ago. We now have to put our paper rolls on covered barges, tow them to Seattle, unload them, then stuff railcars for delivery to the buyer. It's more expensive, of course.

We are looking into buying a small part of the railroad from our mill down to the water in Pt. Townsend where the railcars get loaded onto barges. It will take a few months to see if we can make it work.

An article in the local paper said, "Port Townsend Paper Corp.'s fiber supply and transportation manager, Mary Schroeder said yesterday that if the rail service stops, we're really going to miss it." That's true. The corporation had increased tonnage on the rail line from 40 carloads to 60 per month. "We want the railroad in business so we've been trying to work with it any way we could," she said. "Losing the railroad service would mean more expensive and more inconvenient shipping.

I have been researching the deeds to the railroad property from the mill to the dock and it is very complicated. It seems the landowners who gave the property to the original railroad in the early 1900s did it on one condition, that at some point they connect the railroad with <u>Portland</u>! Wow, that will never happen, but it is one big stumbling block for us, since now the property would logically go back to the heirs of the original owners. I hate to think how much we would spend on attorney's fees just trying to find them.

A pair of Seattle & North Coast F7As uses "reacher" cars to pull freight cars off the float at Port Townsend, Wash., on August 16, 1983. —*Kevin EuDaly photo*

9/13/84

The CZ mill in Port Angeles went on strike just a few days before Labor Day weekend. The mill is still out and the workers are on 12 hours shifts, 10 days on and 4 days off. Not sure how long it will last.

We hired a new log buyer this week. a We are finding it hard to get enough chips and have resulted to chip up a lot of small logs to keep the inventory from going down. We expect to have to do this most of next year, especially after the expansion that starts at the end of next year. I don't have time to also buy logs since it takes a lot of field work. When I convinced Juan we needed a buyer, luckily we found one. It's Rod Quesnel and he has been a log buyer and contract supervisor for Seaboard Lumber for ten years. Seaboard recently went belly up and he will work for them until the end of the year. We agreed to split his salary 50/50 until January 1st when he will work for us full time. I started buying logs a few weeks ago and it put me into major overload.

I guess the chip problem is the hot topic in our company. Everyone is talking about it every day which is why Juan is on my case a lot. He's not the type of person that can ask a question. Instead, he just starts raging about something I did and I'm supposed to start explaining what I did and why. Instead, I tend to get irritated and shut up or ask him why he is so upset, which just makes him more irritated. It's a strained relationship.

He mistrusts everyone and has to make every little decision. Susie finally had it out with him and said she refuses to ask permission to even buy a box of paperclips. He insists on deciding even that!

I remember when I worked for Stoner Lumber in Columbus, Ohio before I went to college. Mr. Stoner had to make every little decision. In a 7-person sales office, 17 people came and went in the 2 ½ years I was there. Four positions changed people four times. I left to go to another job offer and a year later Stoner went bankrupt. The people in a company are its structure, the basic framework of the organization. Stoner finally got what he wanted, people in key positions that couldn't make a decision without his approval. The company grew fast and eventually he couldn't cover all of the bases. The structure crumbled under him and ceased to function. I can see that happening here.

It's only been ten months, but the new mill manger, Truman, already quit because he wasn't allowed to run the mill. Juan called him ten times a day and wouldn't let him manage. Truman was an excellent people manager, tough and demanded accountability from everyone, and everyone respected him. He wasn't Juan's type, but everyone gave Juan credit for having the guts to put someone like Truman in that spot to begin with.

Now, Juan trusts Dick, the Personnel Manager. Dick is very likeable, but most personnel people are. Juan made Dick the new mill manager! The Assistant Manager, Reed Hunt, couldn't handle that since he's been in that position for years and felt he should be manager, so he quit. No love lost there. If you wanted to try anything new, Reed always found a reason it wouldn't work. Remember the movie Officer and a Gentlemen? When the movie producer and stars met with Reed to see if they could make part of the movie in the Port Townsend bag plant, they were all dressed more like the Port Townsend community hippies. Reed hated hippie types, so he said absolutely not. The film company had to make the bag plant scenes at a plant in Tacoma.

Bruce, the Utilities Supervisor in charge of burning hog fuel for energy, has been a favorite of Dicks, so it wasn't surprising that he got the #2 spot of Assistant Plant Manager even though he doesn't know much about paper making. So now Juan can finally run the mill his way through the two people who aren't quite sure what to do themselves. It's real interesting to watch all of this. Dick is now acting a lot like Juan in just ordering people around with no intention to help them do their best. He is getting a big head really quick.

I have been staying in the Winslow office more than usual, so I'm not too involved with mill politics, which is fine with me. This has also helped cool Juan's criticism since here I can run in and ask him about things and get his agreement quickly. Last week I had a big argument with him and I left the office and drove around for two hours trying to decide what to do. I concluded I didn't have to go through all of this hassle anymore and was going to call it quits. I went back to the office and walked into his office fully ready to say "two weeks' notice" or I'd leave that day, but he was on the phone. I went back to my office and cleaned out my desk then the phone started ringing and things started happening. Since it was Friday, I decided to wait until Monday.

By Monday, I decided to get a resume together and look around before quitting. Since then, I've gotten along well with Juan and am slowly preparing data on my accomplishments since Haindl bought the mill. I mentioned my desire to get into transportation management to a few people in the business.

9/23/84

What a fun week! I went to the American Pulpwood Association (APA) convention in Canada. There was an all-day bus tour that took about 75 western chip buyers and chip truckers to a high-tech stud mill, a finger-joint plant where they glue together short pieces of wood to long lengths, a pulp and paper mill, and a logging operation.

On Thursday, there was a technical session where papers on chip related subjects were given. The association is composed of chip buyers, chip truck companies and equipment manufacturers. It was good to hear the other buyers wondering how they would make it through the winter also. They are all going through the same problem, but we had to be extremely careful not to share information.

I volunteered to host the next meeting in spring at Port Townsend. I will be helping organize it with the APA Manager, so maybe I'll be around then if things don't deteriorate too badly with Juan. Maybe I just needed an attitude adjustment.

9/29/84

This week the rumor was that one of my big suppliers that has been shut down is going to start up again. Hooray! That's worth a party! The chip situation has somewhat stabilized. At least we aren't losing ground anymore. I do have to get the inventory up so we can make it through Christmas shutdowns at the sawmills.

Now the pulp and paper market has too much paper, so our orders have dropped off considerably. We may have some mill curtailment. Crazy market—a month ago the paper market was hot and prices were going up. The pressure is off of me a bit and our sales manager, Dave. I think I'll make it!

Tomorrow, I go to Vancouver, Canada with Juan until Wednesday and can't wait to be back home.

10/16/84

The trip to Vancouver with Juan was challenging. He asked the clerk at the hotel to make sure our rooms were next to each other, but when he went to make a telephone call, I changed my room to another floor. This shocked him when he got off the elevator and I told him it wasn't my floor.

That evening we met with the Crown Canada VP in his office suite in Crown's high-rise building downtown. Our meeting was in the VP's official 'sitting room' where we all sat around a beautiful round engraved glass coffee table with crystal bowls on it. As the meeting began, Juan sat cross-legged and kicked his foot up under the glass top, so the whole time we heard the tick, tick, tick of his shoe on the glass. And he smoked the whole time, putting his ashes and finally his cigarettes out in one of the crystal bowls. I just looked at my Canadian counterparts in dismay. Juan didn't care; he was on his game. It's beyond embarrassing, because how he acts doesn't reflect on me.

The next day, my key contact at Crown called me to say the VP told him to never ever do me any favors. We laughed because we know that's not possible in the crazy world of wood fiber, but we got the message.

Our new log buyer, Rod, and I work together really well. At least he's someone who understands logging operations and I can bounce around ideas with him. We are buying all of the logs we can to make into chips. Some days, he just shakes his head at how fast paced this fiber business is compared to just logs. We now have 11 projects to develop new log and chip sources. Some will pay off and some won't. He is now our field person throughout Puget Sound and British Columbia negotiating prices for logs and potential chip supplies.

10/28/84

Only one day out of the office and when I got in the next morning there were 25 telephone messages on my desk. By 5 p.m. I only had 8 left. The pulp and paper market is the weirdest ever. There is tremendous pulp and paper overproduction at a time when prices are diving, while at the same time while sawmills are shutting down left and right. As long as Rod and I keep "turning over stones," I'm confident we'll find enough.

12/4/84

We've moved again. We found a beautiful house to rent on 2 ½ acres with 220' of waterfront on Hood Canal. It is a few miles north of the Bangor Submarine Base, so we get to see all of the Trident nuclear subs come and go.

It's hard to believe, but this is our view, which looks across the canal at the Olympic Mountains, so the sunsets are spectacular when it's clear. Our beach has oysters galore, so with a hammer and bucket, dinner is available in short order. During oyster season we can't seem to eat enough of them.

My first year at Port Townsend Paper has finally settled down and is going quite well. (Am I really crazy or have I just adjusted?) We're all looking forward to our 30% expansion next year. It will be up to Rod and I to find enough chips and logs to make the additional paper.

12/30/84

This New Year is starting off quite different since <u>this is the first letter I've written on the computer.</u> Friends put together eight different programs for us. This one is called Speed Script and lets me just continue to type paragraphs without returning the curser to the next line. It moves a whole word to the next line automatically! They also installed an accounting program that I can use at home. Oops, the program was set up for different size paper, so it's skipped six lines in the wrong places.

At work, Haindl is taking over all of the export orders and transportation arrangements that Crown Zellerbach International was doing for us. To add that on top of everything else has our stress levels off the charts. The union at the mill just reached an agreement with the company after nine months of negotiation. The contract is for two years and begins January lst. The workers are not obligated to join the union. The contract calls for a 1.22% increase in 1985 based on the average of union negotiations at 24 other mills.

1985

1/22/85

At work we're getting ready to reactivate the Crown tugboat named "Diamond Z" to move chip barges in and out at our dock. It is 55' long. Since it will now be owned by a German company, the name of the tug can be changed. Juan is having the name changed to "Mary S."

I told him it sure wouldn't help my popularity at the mill, but of course that didn't faze him. He thinks it's a great name. There are three women named Mary at the mill, so we all use the initial of our last name on everything to keep things straight. Well, it was a good way to prime me for my job review this week. I was prepared and had charts and graphs of my performance in both wood fiber and transportation and reasons why I should get a raise.

Juan, of course, had already made up his mind what I was going to get and so it was like talking to a brick wall. At one point I suggested we make a compromise and he laughed and said there were no compromises. We were both in a good mood so the discussion went well. At one point, he said I was the "damndest, pushiest broad he ever met," but he respected that. Since I spent so much of the company's money, I took it as a compliment.

Then I asked him to tell me how I was doing, good or bad, because I figured there would be some bad. He said I was doing a good job, then changed his mind and said I was doing a hell of a good job. The only bad thing he could think of was that I didn't call enough when I out of town. That means I have to call in three to four times a day when I'm gone. It makes him happy, so that's what I'll have to do.

Then he asked me to tell him what he does that I don't like or if there were any problems. I said since September I have no complaints at all. He said if he ever gets in the way of me doing my job that I shouldn't hesitate to tell him. Wow, what a shock! I guess we're making progress.

My small raise didn't bother me since I'm very happy in my job right now and am focused on the expansion of the mill and the need to find 30% more wood fiber. After I make it through that, my resume will look pretty good. The worst dressing down I received in three months was today when we were discussing the railroad problem. I didn't cut off the discussion early enough and he was pissed that he was going to miss the first few minutes of the Rockford Files on TV at 6 p.m.!

3/3/85

Things at work are rolling right along. We moved into our new office two weeks ago and is it ever nice. I lose track of time since it is such a nice atmosphere.

This past weekend an owner of Haindl Paper was here. The sales manager and finance manager and I had to give presentations on what was happening in our areas of responsibility. The sales manager had a lot of bad news about the prices we're getting for our pulp, since the market is really bad. We had to shut down one of our two machines for a month. The CFO had bad news about the profit level this year due to the bad market.

I then gladly said I would save the company a lot by lowering chip prices in April and I hope to do a lot better than that. After the meeting, I was talking with the owner and he mentioned he had gone helicopter skiing at Whistler near Vancouver, B.C. over the weekend. I asked how he enjoyed it and he replied with his thick German accent, "No one was killed, so it must have been good."

6/10/85

The past two months, my job has been hell. Juan gets on his high horse and can be unbearable, not just to me, but to everyone in the office. Mike, our CFO, and I seem to get the brunt of it because we spend so much of the company's money. Anyway, I was getting myself all worked up over it and could tell I was headed for burnout, in fact a crash and burn. Finally, I concluded that the only way Juan could continue to be such an ass was that he must want me to quit. If I quit, he wouldn't have to pay me severance. Knowing the miser he is, it all seemed logical to me.

Reinhard and I talked about it and he said before I do anything rash, I better go in and have a heart-to-heart talk with Juan. Then we started to figure out how long we could live before we would have to move from this house and sell the boat, etc. He even started clipping food coupons that he always thought was a waste of time. We decided not to sell the boat until we have to.

As I was working to get up my nerve to talk to Juan, my morale was pretty low. I knew if I didn't have the strength and got emotional, it would be all over. He hates weak people and eats them not only for breakfast, but for lunch. Finally, last Thursday I told him I wanted to buy him a couple drinks after work on Friday. He looked at me suspiciously and laughed and said sure. Friday was one of those days where I kept as busy as I could so I wouldn't worry. The worst thing I had to face was if he said yes, he did want me to quit. I'd been working on my resume for a week and it was looking very good, so my confidence level was pretty high.

At 5:10 he came back to my office and said he had to be home by six to see Rockford Files, so I better just talk to him in his office.

That's what I didn't want—to talk to him on his turf. When I went in, he was busy reading his mail and asked what was on my mind.

I said the past two months I could tell we weren't getting along all that great and I finally concluded that the reason was that he must want me to quit. He looked up at me and said, "Jesus, NO!" then he raced to close his office door and starting pacing the room. "Why would you think that?" he asked. I said I'd been at this point before a few years ago and I know the signs—upset stomach, intestinal cramps, loss of energy, heart palpitations, loss of interest in things at home, not wanting to come to work in the morning, and overall being less efficient in my job. I told him if this job continues to affect my health, it isn't worth it.

He said he thought he wasn't the easiest person to work for and I said, "No shit, you're a damned difficult person to work for!" He said he doesn't realize when he's being hard on people and that I am doing one hell of a job and there is no way he wants me to leave. Well, that cleared things up in my mind anyway. Now I know that the next time this harassment starts I can stop it right away, and I will, too.

Then he asked me why some of the people at the mill are quitting. I laid it on the line and told him it's the attitude of management at the mill that treats the people like they're not appreciated and could care less if they're there. People will work for less if they get appreciation. The mill people get neither. He listened is about all I can say. We didn't agree to anything, but I feel much better and our conversations since have been pleasant.

The ironic thing was that same Friday, Susie, his secretary, followed him into his office in the morning and told him she had another job offer and if things didn't change around here, she was going to take it. She is our official office manager, but he has to approve of everything, even the smallest purchase. She laid in on the line that she is not taking it anymore, so he got hit twice in one day. Good thing it was a Friday so he had all weekend to think about it.

Apparently, he went into the office on Saturday and left a lot of work for Susie on Monday. Usually, his notes to her are curt and often rude. On this day the notes were, "Susan, do you think we could…and, I would appreciate it if you would..." Well, we'll see how long this lasts.

When Juan gets too stressed out, he goes duck hunting. He's been hunting a lot lately. Last Monday, Susie asked me to her desk. Juan left a note and a bag of ducks for her on top of the filing cabinet and now blood was running down the side of the cabinet. I was taken back for a minute, then we looked in the bag and there were three dead ducks and they weren't even cleaned.

7/1/85

The weather has been so dry, the driest in 100 years they say. Reinhard has flown every day and sometimes twice a day looking for fires.

Note: I didn't include this in letters to my mother, but I finally realized the wife of a neighbor friend, who was in college, was too often a co-pilot on Reinhard's fire patrol trips.

Last Wednesday, he spotted smoke and called it in before anyone else saw it. Some kids started it accidently with fireworks in a logged off area. The slash or logging residue is bone dry and it could have been a really bad fire. On Thursday, he saw four fires all of which he reported, then gave updates to the ground crews when they arrived.

7/28/85

It hasn't rained for over 6 weeks and the woods are bone dry. Every day the temperature is in the 80-90-degree range. Reinhard continues to fly seven days a week from noon to 5:30 p.m. Today, he spotted another fire and got it taken care of quickly, so only ¼ acre burned. He is worth every penny he charges Crown Z. Everyone is expecting a big fire any day now due to the dryness.

The Mary S.

Remember I was telling you about those PVC's I was having? I think it stands for pulmonary ventricular contractions. The doctor did an echocardiogram to be sure there wasn't a valve problem and there wasn't, thank goodness. He said 50% of the population gets this at one time or another and it almost always goes away through exercise (and I assume less stress).

Yesterday was quite a day for me. The tugboat Haindl finished reconditioning, that used to be called the Diamond Z, is going back into service to shift chip barges back and forth from our unloading dock to the buoys. Juan insisted on renaming it 'Mary S' and I got to christen it! I broke a bottle of champagne on the bow and gave a little speech.

Everyone liked my speech so much they want to get it printed in calligraphy and hang it in the wheelhouse of the tug.

This is what I said:

This tug was built in 1936 and served the Port Townsend mill well for many years before being retired. Now it is infused with a new spirit, the spirit of Port Townsend Paper Corporation.

Changing times demand innovative ideas and the new spirit of Port Townsend Paper Corporation has enabled this tug to be reconditioned and put back into service. May she serve this company well. We ask that the Almighty protect her captain and crew from any perils of the sea. May she always work in calm waters. May the sunshine today be a sign that good fortune will always shine upon her.

Then I smashed the bottle as I said "I christen thee tug, Mary S." and everyone cheered. All of the people in the Winslow office were there as well as some of the friends and relatives of the people who will operate it.

8/10/85

Champion International has had their Tacoma pulp mill for sale for a few months. Haindl was looking at it and hoped to buy it, and then I would again be buying chips for two mills. Juan was hopeful it would all work out. Well, we didn't get it. Juan's good buddy at Simpson Timber bought it. Furman Mosley is the President of Simpson and he and Juan go hunting together, but don't think twice of cutting each other's throat in the business world.

We did our homework, obtained Champion's cost statements, a list of their chip suppliers, and were doing our due diligence and a thorough analysis of the mill. Simpson's team walked through the mill only once, didn't get any financial data, and they bought it. Juan was shocked!

I remember when Haindl was looking at Port Townsend. They went over everything thoroughly and spent a lot of time on wood fiber. I remember one day sitting in a four-hour meeting in front of a team of four chain-smoking bankers being grilled about where the chip supply came from, how secure it was, etc. Simpson didn't even ask for a list of Champion's chip suppliers!

After Simpson signed the deal, I had lunch with Bob Radcliffe, the Champion chip buyer. He had no intention of going to work for Simpson, but if Simpson wanted Champion to supply chips, he would contract to continue to buy them. If Simpson decides to buy the chips themselves, he felt they would run into a lot of problems. Bob told Simpson's negotiators that, next to himself, I was the most qualified person to buy chips for the new company. I already know most of the suppliers and the supply/demand situation in Puget Sound.

Then, I got a call from the person I currently negotiate chip prices with at Simpson's Shelton sawmill, Norm Eveleth. Norm was concerned about the chip supply for the Champion mill and said he wanted to recommend to his boss, Tom Ingham, that I was the best person for the job. Well, I was really touched. I guess that's what most of us work for, recognition by our peers that we are good at what we do.

When Juan was gone last week, I had lunch with the Regional VP of Simpson, Tom Ingham. I have known him for a couple years. Tom said that Simpson didn't want Haindl to have the Tacoma mill, because we would be the only buyer of fir chips and would force the prices down at their sawmill in Shelton. So, they made a tongue-in-cheek offer to Champion knowing they wouldn't take it and "bingo," they accepted it. He said the closing is September 1st, but they are all still in shock that they have just bought the pulp mill. Now isn't that crazy! This might be an excellent opportunity for me to get back into a class company, family-owned, that treats all of their employees as family.

8/22/85

All of a sudden, the transportation person working for me took another job with Louisiana-Pacific in Hayden Lake, Idaho and gave us one-week notice. I've been busy interviewing and covering for his job also. We've had some good candidates and will be doing second interviews soon.

9/5/85

Just our luck, we met a friend whose boyfriend, Kelly, is a lieutenant on the USS Florida, one of the Trident subs. It was family day and crew members could give tours and we were invited as his cousins.

I can't even begin to describe how incredible that sub is. It was on dry dock out of the water. It's four stories high. We had to climb down through the top hatch. We went into every part of the sub, every head, galley, missile bay, torpedo bay, all except the machine room where they keep the electronics in the nosecone. There are 24 missiles and each carries multiple warheads. I think I sent you the newspaper article which tells more than I can remember.

The missiles are kind of scary when you think of the power they have. Kelly is in charge of the missiles and torpedoes. He is a weapons specialist. He just passed his last test and is only one of six people in the US who will be in charge of moving and placing missiles in subs. In a couple weeks, he ends his four years on the sub and becomes an instructor at the base.

Next weekend, we're the Committee Boat again for the Sequim Bay Yacht Club and Sailboat Regatta. This time the regatta will be the day the new marina building is dedicated. John Wayne's family are coming. So far, there are 30 sailboats entered in the race, so we'll have a big job starting races and keeping time. There will be a catered dinner in the club's new quarters that evening and I was asked to be Master of Ceremonies for the award presentation.

9/30/85

The dedication of the John Wayne Marina administration building was quite the affair. John Wayne's daughter, Marissa, came aboard our boat and started the first three races on Saturday, followed by a dinner in the new building attended by over 200 people. Our club hired a band and we danced until 1 a.m.

Sunday, we ran two races and then I ran the awards ceremony. The trophies were walnut plaques mounted with brass laser cut sailboats with a brass plate with the race and place. During the dedication ceremony, each of the Wayne children spoke a few words. Then the VFW presented a flag and as it was raised, they played John Wayne's tape, "America, Why I Love Her" over the loudspeaker and there wasn't a dry eye in the crowd.

Note: Public ad and announcement by Star Marine, Inc.

Star Marine, Inc. is proud to announce expanded operations in the Port Townsend area with the completion of the MARY S. Star Marine's newest tug. Completely rebuilt by company personnel, the 60' steel tug is powered by a fuel efficient 335 hp Caterpillar diesel and has a high-aspect rudder for increased maneuverability.

The MARY S. is also a powerful firefighting platform with a 2000 GPM high pressure fire pump, 3" wheelhouse monitor and 1.5" and 3" deck hoses.

The MARY S. is based in Port Townsend with a local crew to provide fast, dependable service anywhere in the North Puget Sound area.

The MARY S. will be a versatile addition to the company fleet, which includes the 365 HP tug, MALOLO, based in Eagle Harbor and the 150' steel deck barge MAKENA.

Serving the Puget Sound area since 1976, Star Marine offers competitive rates and dependable service in bulk materials transportation, barge shifting, assists, and in moving houses and other large structures.

1986

2/27/86

If anyone would have told me it would take two years to learn how to work with my boss, I would have said they were crazy. Goes to show we never stop learning and running into obstacles we haven't handled before.

The expansion at the mill is going right along, although it is behind schedule so I don't need the extra chip volume until May. The trouble is I am having some glitches in setting up that extra volume, which is an equivalent of 1 ½ barges/week. I'm working with Dunlap Towing to put a chip truck-to-barge reload in their log yard in Olympia. Their log yard has been there for years and there was a sawmill there before that.

The City Planning Commission felt it would be a piece of cake to get the permit to drive a few pilings and float a dock for the barges and put in the conveyor. They approved it. Then the City Council uses an attorney called a Hearing Examiner to take public testimony at a public hearing and rule on the permit. If he said okay, then Council just rubber stamps it. No further testimony is allowed.

Well, welcome to a city where anything goes! The public hearing was expected to last 30-45 minutes, but it lasted 3 ½ hours. About 30 people showed up who live in a residential area on the bluff above the log yard. They had every reason they could think of, irrational and otherwise, why the permit should be denied.

After 10 days, the Hearing Examiner issued his approval with fewer restrictions than the Planning Dept. had originally suggested. Obviously, the facts spoke well for Dunlap. We thought we were home free…well, not quite. The City Council had to concurrently approve the permit at their next meeting. According to their own rules, they use all of the previous testimony in making their decision.

Apparently, the neighborhood group bent the ear of one of the councilmen. When it came up at the meeting, he said there were a lot of problems with it and another hearing would have to be held at another council meeting.

Last Tuesday night, we went prepared. We brought along 8 sawmill owners to speak up for the need of a local reload. The council chambers has about 50 seats, but about 100 people showed up. They were standing three deeps around the inside of the room and were backed up against the doors. My guess was about 60-70 of them were against the permit. There was testimony for 2 ½ hours, split about evenly for and against the reload. Council said they would make a decision by their next meeting in two weeks. So now we wait. It's maddening! If council looks only at the facts they have to approve it, but if they get caught up in the emotional issues, they'll find plenty of ways to deny it.

City of Olympia, WA Planning Commission Map

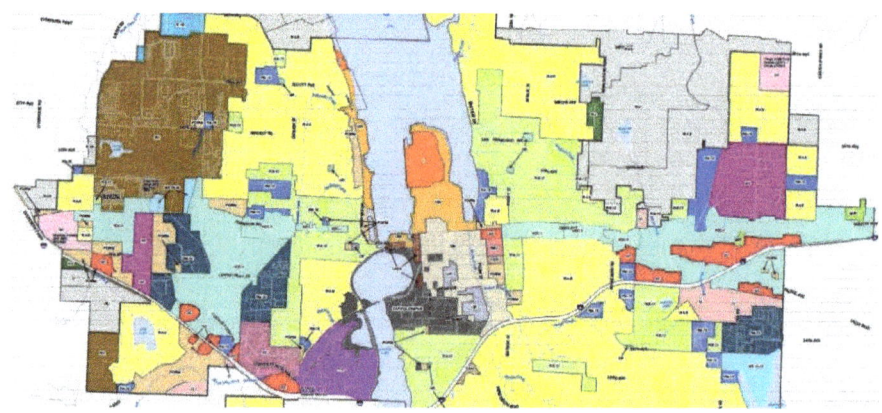

3/19/86

Article in the Olympia newspaper:

THE TERRIBLE STENCH OF FRESH CUT WOOD

The City Council of Camelot-on-the-Bay has ordained another six-week delay in what it laughingly calls the "decision-making process" as to whether tugs and barges can come to town to haul wood chips to the Port Townsend paper mill. They seem to be agonizing over claims that the wood chips cause noxious odors, attract rats, and blow around cluttering up peoples' lawns. I have it on good authority that some West Siders have been warned of genetically mutated rats who prefer a wood chip diet to ice cream and cake. Maybe some of our councilpersons have heard that one and have postponed action while consulting with experts on the *Ratus Norvegius.*

There seems a perfectly logical and convenient way of resolving our city father's and mothers' anxieties over the potentially deadly wood chip. (Wood eating rats spread the bubonic plague). Wood chips are not only being *loaded* and *shipped*, but *produced* in the immediate vicinity of the proposed Dunlap Towing Company facility; at the Delson mill, to be exact. Why not make a field trip from City Hall to West Bay and determine, from personal observation whether the wood chips there produce noxious odors or rats, or blow about polluting the environment? *I have. They don't.*

Fears have also been expressed that the proposed barge terminal would increase "traffic congestion" on West Bay Drive. I drive that thoroughfare daily, and have kept a log of traffic encountered upon it during my last 17 trips from 9 a.m. to 7:30 p.m.. Over the eight days involved I have encountered a total of 96 private vehicles (an average of 5.647 per trip), seven heavy trucks (an average of 0.412

per trip), and two retail delivery vans (an average of 0.117) per trip). At one point I thought I had spotted a Norwegian wood-eating rat, but it turned out to be a miniature dachshund chewing on a rubber bone.

Hundreds of local citizens have signed petitions favoring this job-producing light industry in an area already zoned industrial, including most of the workforce of the local longshoremen's union. They won't be directly involved in the barge loading, but they're smart enough to agree with the sentiments expressed in this column last week: "Delay is the deadliest form of denial!" And the one from the week before "If the decision is to ban this very light industry from an area that has been heavy industrial since 1853, and is so zoned, it will send a warning message to anyone left willing to risk money and a business reputation in trying to bring jobs and expanded tax base to Camelot on Budd Inlet."

Incidentally, the Council might do well to investigate who the individual is who whipped up this neighborhood teapot tempest, and what his motives may be. They would find, I believe, that they aren't altogether altruistic.

Note: The permit was approved!

5/21/86

You've probably heard we're getting some fallout from the nuclear plant disaster in Russia. The newspaper says it's at a low level but readable. It bothers me, but there's nothing we can do. If it wasn't raining so much, it would just continue to float around the world. The comment we hear a lot around here is "Just drink out-of-state beer instead!"

It is almost eerie how little is in the paper about it. Between that and the almost tidal wave, this weather has become quite unusual. By the time we heard a tidal wave was going to hit, it should have already been here. So much for the emergency system. I guess quite a few cities were evacuated to higher ground. I have a friend who is a volunteer fireman in La Conner, north of Seattle on the water. He said people left their homes, but ended up downtown at the tavern on the waterfront. I guess it is hard to relate to a tidal wave.

A yacht club friend who is a VP at Burlington Northern Railroad asked me if I would be interested in serving on the Seattle Emergency Preparedness Committee organized by the city. He has been on it for a year now and they are bogged down in arguing about what to do if an atomic bomb hit Seattle. You won't believe this, but one of their top ten solutions is to put people on ferries and send them to the Olympic Peninsula! Unbelievable!

Not long ago, one of the ferry captains steered the Winslow ferry too close to shore so he could wave to his girlfriend and it went aground. One of the passengers immediately got out a gun and tried to take over the ferry. I don't think I have time to sit in an office in Seattle and brainstorm what to do if a bomb went off. It would just be chaos.

10/5/86

About three weeks ago, Juan and I had dinner with our biggest domestic supplier. The reason for the dinner was my recommendation that the supplier confront Juan about their difficulty in negotiating prices with me, when Juan keeps changing his mind on our position. I told the supplier to be very frank with Juan and to ask him if they should be dealing directly with him, because every time I meet with them and think we have it all ironed out, Juan changes his mind and we have to start all over again.

During dinner, Juan was just smooth as silk, friendly, just a great guy so nothing was said about this issue. But three times during the evening, Juan made inappropriate comments about me and I told him point blank that if he wanted to discuss that, we could do it tomorrow, but this wasn't the place. Finally, the supplier jokingly said he hoped I would still be with the company in the morning, since I was cutting off whatever off-color discussion Juan was trying to start. Then I had to bring up the real purpose of the meeting since the supplier was obviously not going to and we got it semi-ironed out.

By the time dinner was over and we were back at the office it was midnight and Juan had had his five Dr. Nelsons (half vodka, half gin) and was blitzed, although still very sharp. I headed for my car wanting to get the hell out of there when he said. "I want to talk to you." And I knew what was coming. I was ready and glad. It was all going to be over; I could go on with my life, the worst would be over. Then he leaned up against the building and said, "I want to know why you are unhappy with your job." I about fainted. I was speechless. I asked what he meant and he said he felt I was unhappy and that was the last thing he wanted and what could he do to make things better. Then I just let go and told him all about the things that bugged me.

He said he knew I had had other bad bosses. I said yes, but when I did, I knew sooner or later they would be transferred or promoted. So, he asked if I am hoping he will kick the bucket! I said no, but I have had some damn good bosses and I really miss the interface and information sharing and brainstorming. He said from now on if he starts hassling me or interferes with my ability to do my job that I should tell him and he will try to change. We shook hands on it. Now I just have to wait and see what happens.

Our relationship has been great since then, but we have a chip shortage again due to the strike at the Canadian sawmills. As soon as we have a high inventory or prices start going up, it will be another acid test.

11/1/86

This week I have to go to Vancouver BC again for a couple of days. The International Woodworkers of America's sawmill strike in British Columbia is still going on. I've been able to buy 26 barges of chips from Canadian sawmills over the past three weeks. The reason the barges were available is that the union forbid the non-union operating Canadian sawmills from delivering chips to British Columbia pulp mills, so their only choice is to export chips to the US. It's been a real windfall for us.

11/17/86

The Canadian strike continues since July 23rd and our biggest fir supplier down here went on strike last week. It's been crazy. Juan has been great ever since our talk, so it's an improvement. We have two of the owners here from Haindl in Germany, and they are not too happy about how things are going. I didn't know that <u>we'd spent $25 million on the expansion since the beginning of the year and had not produced one extra ton.</u> Now I know why Haindl is truly upset. We were supposed to expand production one-third from 150,000 to 200,000 ton/year. This has been the hottest pulp market in a couple of decades, and we're missing it.

12/21/86

Just before vacation this summer, I received a call from a headhunter trying to fill a job in the wood fiber business in California. My name was given to him by another chip buyer who knew how stressed I was in my job.

I submitted my resume and then had an interview in Portland with the headhunter. A few days later, he told me to expect a call from another officer in the company sometime next week. On Wednesday night, the officer called, and we talked for an hour and a half. It ended with a tentative agreement for me to meet upper management at their corporate office in LA during the first week in January.

The job would be in northern California, probably based in Redding. The company is Pacific Lighting Energy Systems, a subsidiary of Pacific Lighting Corporation (a holding company) whose subsidiaries include Southern California Gas, the nation's largest gas utility, which supplies gas to the whole LA area, Thrifty Drug Stores, Terra Resources, which explores for oil and gas in 16 states, and much more.

Pacific Lighting has three main areas of business: geothermal steam to make electricity, interstate and offshore natural gas pipelines, and alternative energy systems making electricity from steam or hydro, landfill gas, and waste wood, which is where I would come in.

In northern California, Pacific Lighting owns a 16-megawatt power plant in Oroville that makes electricity out of waste wood. They are partners in two other wood-fired plants in Burney and Westwood. Since they're already involved in buying waste wood, Pacific Lighting thought it would be a great opportunity to guarantee the wood supply for the new 50 MW wood-fired plant in Anderson, California, for a fee. Construction of the plant was just beginning, and it would be operational by the end of 1987.

Signal Energy is building the plant and has already signed a contract with Pacific Lighting to supply the wood. I guess the rationale for Pacific Lighting was to be in control of the wood flow in that area. But by the time they decided to interview me, they had surprisingly found out that:

1) they have no one in their company who knows how to go about developing the wood supply;

2) the fiber buyer they had at their own plants was not doing a good job;

3) the new plant was going to come online in a few months, and if they can't supply enough wood at the right price, they are faced with hefty penalties, and

4) they desperately need someone in charge who has experience in the field of Wood Fiber Supply to walk in and do the job.

The person in Pacific Lighting in charge of their wood-fired power plants had been in the position only four months. He knew nothing about wood fiber supply. The consultant they used to find a buyer for this position was the person I talked to on the phone. It was obvious he knew just a tiny bit more about the scope of the business. Finally, they concluded that providing Signal with the wood fiber might be more complicated than anticipated and could cost them A LOT in penalties. Signal then bought Wheelabrator Fry, Inc. in 1983, which became Wheelabrator Technologies, a subsidiary of Waste Management in 1985. The plant was renamed Wheelabrator Shasta Energy.

1987

Early January 1987

I flew into LAX for an interview with Pacific Lighting and their consultant in their Commerce office. I wasn't sure how far it was from the airport, so I took a taxi and it cost $75. Wow! Luckily, I did have enough cash to get back to the airport.

Before I went to the interview, I contacted my colleagues in the chip and fuel business to get up to speed on what they knew about the volume of waste wood production in California. Corky Cornwall at Louisiana Pacific in Eureka, Phil Morgan at Louisiana Pacific in Antioch, and Bob Coffman at Weyerhaeuser Corporation in Klamath Falls were not involved in the California market but were very helpful.

My interview with Lee Freeman of Pacific Lighting and his consultant lasted a little over <u>eight hours</u>. I went in with the attitude that I was there to help them understand the business and if I got the job, it would be fine.

We went over the consultant's report, which said there was more than enough wood supply within a 90-mile radius of this $100 million plant to fulfill their needs for years. I wanted to be sure that they really did buy into the report before I had to bust their bubble. I felt so compassionate for them that I wanted to be as honest as I could to show them how the wood fiber business operates.

The map of the wood fiber basket for this new plant was not a 90-mile radius, but the area from Washington, Oregon, and down to the middle of California. I shared a list of sawmills in the area of the new plant, production rates, transportation routes, and everything I could think of to show them the consultant's report was delusional. At the end of eight hours, we were all exhausted, so I went home and left them with a lot to ponder.

Unfortunately, there were major errors in the original consultant's report, such as:

1) The Forest Service owns almost 50% of Shasta County, where the plant would be located, and although they offer timber sales, any additional wood is difficult to get off of federal land;

2) The current volume of fuel on the market was currently being used, which means the supply would have to be taken away from current users or developed from some currently unknown sources, i.e., higher prices;

3) A lot of the volume the consultant said was available was wood chips being used for pulp and paper, and, yes, there were additional chips not being used locally, but they were being sold at much higher prices on the export market through the port in Eureka to Japanese pulp mills.

There was one bright light. Sierra Pacific Industries was constructing a high-tech sawmill in Anderson, just a few miles from the project, and there was a chance that fuel could be purchased. But, if Sierra Pacific had fifteen loads a day of hog fuel available, it wouldn't put a dent in the 100 loads a day needed by the new power plant by a long shot. I redrew the 90-mile radius to include the whole West Coast and explained that the wood basket is the West Coast. I drew arrows to show how market forces shift availability and how and where the wood supply currently goes. They were amazed and, thank goodness, worried.

The day after I got home, Pacific Lighting offered me the job. It would start in February and pay $65,000 plus bonuses (assuming they would get a bonus under their current agreement with Signal, which I knew was likely impossible). I would be the head of a separate wood fiber supply company that would be set up to protect Pacific Lighting from the massive penalties in their contract. I would set up the company myself to be called Pacific Wood Supply, and my boss would be in Los Angeles. The main and immediate goal was to develop the wood supply for the Signal power plant, which will use 400,000 BDT/s per year which is a significant increase over the amount of fuel I've been buying.

The way I saw it, the plant would come online at the end of 1987. To develop the wood supply contracts and get it flowing would be a great challenge. After a year, it will be fully operational, and then I can come back to Puget Sound and do something else. Northern California is not the greatest place in the world to live—lots of National Forest land, damp on the coast, hot in the interior with lots of wildfires, and a lot of small towns. Reinhard thinks it would be a great opportunity for me, which is true.

Note: Letters to Mother did not contain the fact that Reinhard and Joanna were now in a deep ongoing relationship. I remember vividly when I came home from one of my 12-hour days to see two lawn chairs in the backyard with sunscreen and beach towels and two empty wine glasses in the dishwasher. I said I'd reached my limit in this situation. But then two days later, when I got home late and asked about his day, he said he and Joanna flew to the San Juan Islands for lunch. Now, that was it. I'm done working this hard to support their relationship. He said he couldn't quit, so now it was clear that I could truly quit this 21-year marriage with clarity.

The following week I told Rod about my new job and asked him to go with me when I told Juan. He thought that was a good idea. I didn't need a lecture or a rampage on why I was moving on. I told Juan I needed to talk with him, and when he was ready, Rod and I went in, and I shut the door. I said I had a wonderful job opportunity and would be leaving in two weeks. He looked up, and all he said was, "Why is Rod here?" I said because Rod would be taking over my work until my replacement could be found. All he said was, "Okay." What a relief! But from that moment on, he quit speaking to me.

1/31/87

The office had a luncheon for me with very thoughtful gifts, and Juan just sat in his office and ignored me.

Transportation companies and suppliers held a fabulous party for me at the Poulsbo Yacht Club that I'll never forget that included several vases of red roses. Bob Radcliff from St. Regis Paper read his infamous story "My Dog named Sex" by Carl Papa Palmer, and had everyone doubled over laughing. Note: Today you can find it on google.

Puget Sound Freight Lines managers brought a huge heavy plywood box 8'x4' with chains all over it with signs "Wild Animal – Stay Away." They jiggled and jostled the box into the building, and everyone was nervous. Then Herb Stepper brought in a huge chainsaw, started it up, and cut off the top of the box…sawdust flying everywhere. He pulled out the cutest teddy bear, dressed in blue jeans, a vest with the Puget Sound logo, and a Puget Sound ballcap. Today, I still have him. Adorable!

Friends from the pulp mill gave a big introduction to their gift of the world's only true chipper, a beautiful Haida carving of a beaver. In Haida, it symbolizes resilience and resourcefulness, which is so perfect for what this job required. The evening was topped off by another huge box brought into the room by a couple of suppliers with a ribbon on top that… once it was opened… contained a male stripper! Oh my, and I still have his underwear. It was an evening no one will forget!

2/7/87

I left Seattle with five suitcases, but only two arrived in Redding, so I had to go shopping. I think I'm going to like it here—nothing but sunshine! The first day, I rented a car and drove all over to get a feel for the area. I've been staying at the Red Lion, a very nice motel, and looking for an apartment and office space.

3/12/87

I moved into my office today. It took five trips from the apartment to the car and the same from the car to the office just to move the paperwork, and it was pouring buckets. I rented office furniture and have just one room in a series of suites with a common receptionist. They bill me once a month for all office services.

As soon as I find my #2 person and a clerk, we'll move out of this office, and I'm not sure exactly where we will be. I was in LA three days this week, so it doesn't leave much time to make all of that happen.

The contract Pacific Lighting signed with Signal Energy Systems requires that we, Pacific Wood, a subsidiary of Pac Lighting, buy all of the wood for the plant. The planned startup is December 1987. It will use about 400,000 BDTs/year or about 100 semi-truck loads/day, seven days/week.

The people who negotiated the contract put some really stupid things in it for both companies, so my boss, Lee, said my first assignment was to renegotiate the Signal contract to eliminate the penalties. This would be an opportunity to save our company a few million in potential penalties in case I'm not successful, so Pac Lighting's president is watching this closely. It will probably take a couple of months since the Signal people are in New Hampshire and only get out to the plant every other week. I feel really good about it and think I'll be successful, although being successful could mean I'll be out of a job!

In the meantime, I'm now in charge of the wood supply for the Oroville power plant, and it was very obvious that the fiber buyer needs to be replaced. Every time I talk to accounting, they tell me of another screwball deal he made. He buys shavings and sells them for less than we paid for them. He runs a Trommel system to make usable fuel out of log yard waste, which costs us double what we can buy on the market. It goes on and on. As soon as our #2 person is on the job, I want him on top of the situation since I'm too swamped at the moment to deal with it.

We own two-thirds of two other 10 MW power plants in Burney and Westwood, CA. The partner who has one-third operates the plants and buys the wood. Neither plant is making a profit, but in the world of power, they are in their infancy stage, only two years old with a life span of 30 years. Pac Lighting has decided to take over operations and purchase wood, effective July 1st.

This added two more plants to my list of responsibilities:

	MWE	MBDT/YR
Wheelabrator	50	400
Oroville	18	144
Burney	10	80
Westwood	10	80

Total 704 MBDT/year equivalent to 70,400 truck/year or 192/day.

Our territory for buying wood is all of northern California (which is as large as the State of Washington) and southwest Oregon, but in a pinch it could include northern Oregon and all of Washington.

So far, the people I'm working with are just great. I seem to fit right into the mold, I guess. Pacific Lighting is so young—only 2 years old—and is going through a lot of growing pains. The staffing level in Commerce went from 40 to 120 in one year! There are opportunities everywhere I look.

Photo of Burney Forest Power

6/17/87

Hope you can read this since it's printed on the office computer. If I knew how to double the size of the print, it would look better. Maybe by the next time I write, I'll have mastered more of this program, Microsoft Word.

I had been asking around who might be a great log buyer for Pacific Wood, and Tad Mason's name came up several times. He was working for P&M Cedar at the time. He saw the Signal project as an exciting opportunity that doesn't come along very often and was happy to join our fledgling team.

Work continues to be very hectic but fulfilling. Many items that I have been working on for a few months are finally moving along. Having Julie (accountant) and Tad (log buyer) has helped a great deal. Since the previous buyer is finally gone at Oroville, Tad has been spending a lot of time there cleaning up the problems. Now, we'll be making some real progress.

Sierra Pacific is not interested in selling us wood fuel from their new sawmill and is holding out for a much larger price. They don't think we'll have enough, and a shortfall means higher prices. Our strategy is to fill the yard up with cull logs and chip them if we have to.

Signal agreed to purchase a drum chipper and associated equipment to process the cull logs. The drum is quite large, but perfect for the size of the logs we had to put through it.

7/3/87

I had a wonderful week in Southwest Oregon. I have five meetings scheduled over 2 ½ days. We are getting close to starting fuel deliveries at Signal and plan to start accepting logs on July 20th. Tad is working hard to get log volume under contract.

We have been meeting with Signal management and they have not been as cooperative as one would expect. They prefer that we do not bring in any wood until they need it, but that is totally unrealistic. There is not much logging around here in the winter, which means building a log inventory is done during the summer months. They say the plant is about one month ahead of schedule, which makes it even more imperative that we take deliveries this month. I don't know what they think they would burn if we waited until the last minute to bring in fuel.

The ex-fuel buyer from Oroville still pops up once a week or so. If I was prone to heartburn, I surely would have it by now. I visited a supplier last week who was not sending us all of his waste wood. He said the previous buyer was reselling some of it to another buyer, which was our competitor. By the end of our meeting, he agreed to sell the balance to us and insisted on getting someone else to haul it besides the ex-buyer's buddy.

In Oregon, I visited a competitor's power plant to see how they were doing with their wood inventory. The buyer introduced me to the plant manager, who said, "So you work for (our ex-buyer)," and I was more than happy to clarify his misconception. Apparently, the ex-buyer visited him a week or so ago and left the impression that he still worked for us, and I worked for him. What a guy!

8/1/87

LETTER TO FRIENDS ABOUT MY MOVE

Greetings from sunny California!

Yes, believe it or not, I have a new address in one of the warmest places around this time of year, Redding, CA. I moved here in February to take on the job of Director of a subsidiary company called Pacific Wood Fuels. The parent is Pacific Lighting Energy Systems out of Commerce, CA.

It all started in early December with a call from a headhunter. I had been looking around for opportunities, but never considered leaving the Northwest. This was an offer I just could not pass up—to start up a new company and be in charge of my own business. The key task is to develop and supply the wood for a 50-megawatt power plant being built eight miles south of town by Signal Energy. It will start up in December and need 100 semi-truckloads of wood every day, seven days a week, to produce electricity. In addition, I'm already responsible for providing wood to another Pacific Lighting power plant in Oroville, CA, 18 megawatts in size. In November, I'll be responsible for two more of their power plants in Burney and Westwood, CA, each 10 megs in size.

I hired a log/fuel buyer and an office manager to help with all of this. In about a month, I hope to hire an additional fiber buyer. There's not much excess wood around here, so we have to develop it with loggers and chippers and then outbid other power plants and pulp mills. It's going to get very interesting between now and year-end.

I have a lovely apartment overlooking the city. It's very unusual to live alone after 21 years, but it's kind of adventurous, too. Work takes up most of my time, as you can imagine. Long hours and 7-

day work weeks. I have joined a writer's club. Writing is something I've wanted to do more of for a long time. I'm trying my hand at writing a screenplay. With all of the experience I have in this crazy wood business, I have plenty of stories to share.

Mother came out to visit for two weeks in May. It was 100 degrees all but two days. We drove to the coast and through some of the redwood groves. We even went to a rodeo, Lake Shasta, and Mt. Shasta. It did hit 114 degrees one day in June, but most of the time, it's between 90-100. Very dry heat, so it's easy to get used to. It's the sunshine every day that keeps my energy level up.

Just wanted to let you know what is going on. Reinhard decided to stay in Washington and build his flying business. He is at the same address. Best wishes, Mary

Mt. Shasta   Shasta Lake

Whiskeytown Lake

8/6/87

This past week, we sent out announcements that we are now in the business of buying cull logs (that can't be made into lumber) at the power plant. TV Channel 7 and Channel 24 showed up to film our first log truck delivery, and the Redding Record Searchlight newspaper had a nice article on it. We will eventually chip the logs and burn the wood to produce electricity.

Tad, Julie, Mary, and Joe Cheek,
the owner of Cheek Logging who brought
in the first load of cull logs

Soon, Signal asked for a meeting to notify us the plant was going to start up two months early! They expected us to be aghast, but all I said was, "Great!" and then we scrambled. We were able to fill the storage yard with a large cull log inventory, which gave us leverage to negotiate low hog fuel prices. Things were looking really good.

The day before plant startup, we had arranged for 175 truckloads of hog fuel to be delivered (almost two days-worth of usage). The plant had installed three truck dumps that lifted the whole van and trailer into the air. The fuel falls out into a bin, where it's metered onto a conveyor belt that moves it 200 yards to the storage pile.

I'll never forget how excited we were about bringing that number of truckloads in one day ahead of startup. What perfect timing. The scale house was staffed and ready to not only weigh the trucks in and out, but to take samples of the wood fuel and dry it overnight to determine the moisture content. Wood fuel is typically purchased on a bone-dry ton basis, so the moisture content is tested and price adjusted.

Late in the afternoon the day before deliveries began…it was 4:00 p.m. exactly when Bill Carlson, the plant manager, called to notify me that: 1) A welder working on the truck dumps caught the conveyor belt on fire, and 2) they would not be able to unload any trucks! And 3) the conveyor belt was one of a kind, and it would take at least a month to get a new one!

After the initial shock, Tad and another recent hire, Milt Schultz, and I got on the phones and hunted down all of the self-unloading vans we could find in Washington, Oregon, and California. The trucking companies helped us a lot to place self-unloading vans at many of our supplying sawmills to keep them from shutting down. These vans are also called 'walking floors' that move the fuel out of the van onto the ground near the fuel pile. Then our front-end loader pushed the fuel onto the stockpile.

Then we were lucky to find and rent two portable truck dumps that we set up near the fuel pile the next day. These can lift up those trailers that did not have 'shuffle' floors. Not the truck and trailer, just the trailer. It was costly, but it was an emergency. Our first day of purchasing a sawmill's wood waste and we forced them to shut down! Oh, no, we weren't going to let that happen. It would take months to regain their trust, but also their loss of revenue from lumber production.

We didn't get any sleep that night, but we made it work. What a rush, yet it was just another day of spur-of-the-moment negotiations in the volatile business of wood fiber supply.

Wheelabrator Shasta Energy under construction

One of three truck dumps installed to unload 100 loads/day

Epilogue:

OF COURSE, IT'S POSSIBLE!

A. BARGING CHIPS FROM CANADA

With the additional demand for wood waste for Signal's 50 MW wood-fired power plant, it wasn't long before there was a severe shortage of chips, sawdust, and hog fuel that impacted at least seven of the wood-fired power plants in northern California.

Coming from Puget Sound, I talked with a couple of chip and wood waste buyers to kick around the potential for buying chips and wood waste in British Columbia, Canada. It would be loaded onto an ocean-going barge in Vancouver and delivered to a port to be determined in the Bay Area. We brought in some other buyers and decided it was worth a try.

Dave Allen and I negotiated a deal with Fletcher-Challenge's Canadian sawmills to load wood waste into a Crown Canada ocean-going barge to be towed by Seaspan International. The barge held 12,000 tons of wood waste, or 480 truckloads. We worked with the Levin-Richmond Terminal (near Oakland) to set up a reload for the wood waste to then be loaded into trucks and delivered to seven wood-fired power plants in Central California. It didn't solve the shortage problem, but it energized everyone's mind in finding creative ways to fill the wood fiber gap.

Photo: Seaspan barge from Canada

Departed Vancouver, B.C. December 2, 1989

Arrived Port of Richmond, California on December 6, 1989

Fuel Source: Fletcher-Challenge Canadian sawmills

Carrier: Seaspan International, Vancouver, B.C.

Payload: 12,000 tons or 480 truckloads

Purchaser: Ultra Power Biomass Fuels Corporation,

Auburn, California

Destination: Levin-Richmond Terminal

Recipients of the Fuel:

Left to right: Tony Wetzel (Ultrapower): R. H. "Corky" Cornwall (Louisiana-Pacific); Mary Schroeder (Pacific Wood Fuels); Phil Morgan (Gaylord Container); Mike McCoy (Levin-Richmond); Dave Allen (Ultrapower); Jack Frost (San Francisco Bay Tug Pilot); John Barker (Seaspan); Steve Wickson (Bobell Ltd.); Murray Hall (Fletcher-Challenge); and Dave Bischel (Ultrapower).

B. OTHER CREATIVE IDEAS

Another time, I received a call from a logger in Montana who said they were overloaded with wood waste and asked if there was a way to get it to northern California. When I visited his operation, I was surprised at how much wood waste was stockpiled, and luckily it was located near a railroad line. I talked with Burlington Northern, who used the railroad line, about loading the wood waste onto their rail cars. The closest they could deliver it to us was Burney, the end of their line. We set up a loading ramp in Montana and a reload in Burney, and for many weeks, we moved the wood waste through the reload onto trucks for Signal and the other plants we supplied.

Early on, when I met with the management team of the Shasta-Trinity National Forest, one of the foresters asked if I was "Doghair Mary," the person they had read about in timber magazines, and I blushed. Yes, which helped build enthusiasm for experimenting with using portable chippers on logging sites based on the experiments we did in Puget Sound. What fun it was to expand the sources of wood waste and be able to fully serve Signal and the other plants I was responsible for. (See the appendix for more details.)

Other creative ideas included letting landowners bring in tree trimmings that we would throw in with logs that we chipped, which still continues.

One time, when Simpson's Pulp Mill (not even a quarter mile from Signal) had bales of pulp they couldn't sell, we brought in a tub grinder to see if we could grind the bales into pieces that would go through Signal's conveyor system and make it to the boilers. When the grinder started, it took less than a minute to watch the pulp bales break and be thrown twenty feet in the air, and a thousand pieces went everywhere. We had a good laugh about that as it took a few hours to clean up that mess.

There are thousands of acres of fruit orchards in California, which annually tree their trees. Trimmings on the ground are typically piled and burned. It isn't perfect, but small chippers moving through the orchards were tried and worked in some cases.

As time went on, the market volatility mellowed out. Tad was offered a position with a consulting firm, and Milt retired. I was able to hire Steve Jolly, one of Roseburg Lumber's log buyers, to fill their spots, and Signal offered to handle all of our paperwork and phone calls with one of their excellent office staff members, Kay Hutsell. We were a great team.

C. WASHINGTON, D. C. 1992

The Forest History Society's records show that the U.S. Fish and Wildlife Service (FWS) officially listed the northern spotted owl as threatened under the Endangered Species Act on June 23, 1990. There was a delay in ordering any specific management plan, because of the immediate impacts that the ruling might have on the timber industry.

When it looked like the impact of protecting the northern spotted owl would decimate the California timber and wood products industry, the whole region was in an uproar. Managers and foresters from local sawmills held dozens of meetings to not only find common ground, but come up with options for federal land managers to consider.

In Hayfork, local women formed a group called "Women in Timber" to help save the sawmill in the community. Nadine Bailey, the wife of a logger, became the spokesperson for the group. Nadine and I became fast friends as we often attended and spoke at the same public meetings regarding the implications of the owl's listing. At one point, we were invited to the Canadian Timber Association's annual meeting in Vancouver, Canada, to share with the Canadian mill owners how the listing of the owl was impacting the industry in northern California that eventually might impact their forest land.

In 1992, Vice President Dan Quayle came to Anderson to meet with industry leaders at the Roseburg Lumber Company office. Nadine Bailey and I had been a local voice for many of the mills with the media and making presentations to the Forest Service at their public hearings. We were invited by S.H.A.R.E., a group of mill managers, lumber companies, and local business representatives, to make the industry's presentation to the Vice President. Left: I'm in the blue suit on the left, Nadine in the black suit to my right.

Right: Myself, V.P. Quayle, and Bill Carlson, Signal General Manager

A week later, I received a call from V. P. Quayle's office inviting Nadine and I to come to Washington, D. C., and make the same presentation to his staff members in the Old Executive Office Building who were working with FWS on the spotted owl issue.

About 7 p.m. the night before making our presentation, I received a call from a D.C. environmental group president (I can't remember who) and he was highly upset that we were in town to make this presentation. He was livid that no one from Signal Energy had notified him and he felt our presentation would negatively impact all of the work they were doing for the environment. I told him that we had already made the presentation to V. P Quayle and that the message was powerful enough that he invited us here. This president was adamant that we would not make the presentation, but I said that if he understood what we were presenting, he would also like it.

Now yelling at me, he demanded that I immediately come to his office and show the presentation to their management team. I said I was not dressed appropriately, but he didn't care if I was even in my pajamas, but be there within a half an hour! I didn't bother Nadine, since this was a Signal Energy issue. I took a cab to his office with my presentation items and was immediately ushered into a room with this president and four managers. No introductions, the president said, "Just get on with it."

I set up the presentation and made my case, after which the five went into another room to discuss it. When the president came back in, he said it was okay and they approved. Although the information in our presentation was good, and the options I presented were already being used to protect other endangered species, so why make protections for the owl so severe? But our proposal had no impact on the decisions. While in Washington, we also made our presentation to our local congressman and senator. They were grateful to be kept informed.

In 2022, an article in the California Globe, written by Kevin Nelson, stated that **"In the 1980s, California was a superstar timber producer. Nearly 150 sawmills churned out four billion board feet of lumber every year, leading the nation." In 2023, only 29 California sawmills were active.** The loss of thousands of jobs was the real impact of listing the spotted owl and the implementation of the USFWS management plan.

D. MOVING FROM WOOD WASTE TO CONSERVATION PROJECTS

Realizing the wood fiber business was taking an increasing toll on my health, in 1998, I left and went to work for a friend's publishing company for a few months. Then, the head of the City of Anderson's Planning Department asked if I would help for a few months on a special project relating to grant reporting. It was great fun, and what a wonderful group of people. I always smile when I think of them.

It wasn't long before a surprising opportunity came along. In 1999, I accepted the position of District Manager of the Western Shasta Resource Conservation District (RCD), a 1.7-million-acre special district of the state that specialized in stream restoration, fuels reduction, and water and conservation projects, all funded through competitive grant programs.

When I began, the RCD had three employees: Jeff Souza, Project Manager, and two project workers. It was a time when federal and state agencies began offering millions of dollars for environmental projects.

My main focus was writing grant applications (which for several years had a 60% success rate), completing detailed reports on the implementation of each grant, and accountability for the funds spent. Jeff's focus was planning the implementation of each piece of the project puzzle with field staff, supervising and overseeing the work completed, and making sure it met the specific expectations and was within the budget of the grant contract.

The district had just been awarded a $1.5 million grant for the first of many restoration projects for Lower Clear Creek. This prominent creek had been decimated by gold mining in the last century and previously was a valuable spawning ground for winter-run salmon.

Jeff had brought together managers from various state and federal agencies to form a Technical Advisory Committee (TAC) to plan the restoration projects to restore habitat for the winter salmon run. The TAC's express purpose was to create a master plan to restore about six miles of Lower Clear Creek from Whiskeytown Dam to the Sacramento River.

Over the next ten years, this excellent document enabled the RCD to receive over fifty grants that totaled over $15 million from a multitude of agencies for identified projects in the master plan. All were successfully completed, and the best news is it returned the health of Lower Clear Creek so that it once again attracts a significant winter-run salmon population. All of the people involved in the restoration were thrilled when it was announced that The Lower Clear Creek Floodway Rehabilitation Project received the prestigious 2006 California Governor's Environmental and Economic Leadership Award for its successful conservation efforts.

According to a 2025 update by the Bureau of Land Management, the comeback of Lower Clear Creek's salmon run is holding, and fish can be seen in fall and winter from the Bureau's Clear Creek

Gorge overlook, about seven miles west of Redding Rancheria along Clear Creek Road.

Recently, Jeff reminded me how lucky we were to have such a talented board of directors who ran our district, a government organization that was more like a business. The directors were willing to take some well-thought-out strategic risks when other RCDs were more risk-averse, although there was a lot of available funding at the time. How lucky we were to hire Megan, Paula, Christy, Todd, Hide, John, Candy, Priscilla, Leslie, Maureen, Ryan, and many others. And then how crushed we felt each time one of those great folks left to move on to bigger and better things.

Crushed is a good word for how it felt, but it wouldn't be long before we'd be very proud of them as they made good use of the training they received at the RCD for further promotions and success. And it wouldn't be long before another enthusiastic person walked in, ready to join the team and learn the ropes. There was so much to learn.

Implementing on-the-ground projects based on the technical requirements the TAC spelled out and the agencies included in the grant contracts, as well as the extensive reporting requirements, was often a heavy load for all of us.

When I was ready to retire from the district in 2012, there were at least three dozen projects underway, not only in the Clear Creek watershed but also in watersheds like Cow Creek, Middle Creek, and Churn Creek. And the grant funds awarded to the RCD at that time to implement those projects exceeded $3 million dollars.

E. ON TO MINISTRY, SPIRITUAL DEVELOPMENT, AND FINDING MY SOULMATE

A quick backup: In 1989, after two years of working 60-70 hours a week at Signal Energy, I felt it was time to meet people in the greater community. I decided one way was to attend the Women's Refuge Annual Crab Feed.

I wore my best suit with a high collar and when I went to the bar to order a glass of wine, the barmaid said, "This must be your first time out." All I could do was choke out, 'Yes, how did you know?" She laughed, got me a glass of wine and told me to follow her. She introduced me to a large table of her single friends. They were all so friendly, it was quite a relief!

As we all talked, this was a group of people from the Center for Spiritual Living in Redding. In early discussions, having been raised Catholic, I was immediately attracted to these teachings that were drawn from the world's wisdom and traditions that are considered spiritual, not religious. The next morning, I attended my first service at the Red Lion Hotel and, I swear, the minister was speaking only to me! I knew this philosophy of positive living was for me. It's funny that the experience of being spoken to directly by the minister happen a lot when people first attend.

I began taking classes and was eventually licensed as a prayer practitioner (two years of classes), then received a ministerial license (another two years of classes) and later a doctorate (several years of volunteer work for the organization, which for me was seven years of writing monthly articles on the power of positive living for their "Creative Thought Magazine," and writing six books. Today, I continue to teach classes and serve the Center and the congregation.

In 1991, not having anything in particular to do on the Sunday of Memorial Weekend, after service I invited many people to my house for brunch. To my amazement, about twenty people showed up! Luckily, Dan Ducheneau, a local TV chef, came and he chased me out of the kitchen so I could talk to everyone while he concocted an amazing brunch.

One of the men who came was Paul Mitchell. I didn't get to talk to him that day, but I found out later that he was very impressed with the high-end stereo system I had as well as my house that I had recently built. A week later he called to invite me to a poetry potluck at his place in Igo, about 10 miles west of Redding. I was intrigued, since I don't like and don't understand poetry, but it was another opportunity to meet people. He said he would mail me a map of how to get to his 15-acre property on Zogg Mine Road.

The morning of the poetry potluck, I had my hair done and shared my reluctancy about going to a poetry event with my hairdresser. He said "No problem, just buy a book of Robert Service poems and you'll be fine." Next stop was Barnes & Noble and I found his poetry, but it was all bar room poetry! Whoa! I don't even know who Paul Mitchell is and I don't want to offend anyone. I bought the book feeling confident it would have something in it I could use.

A couple of hours later, I was still looking for the right poem and finally decided, based on what I was learning about positive thinking, this must be a God thing. I come from a mid-Ohio beer drinking family. Every family gathering always had a keg of beer, lots of food, and singing old songs. So, the poem I chose was "Lipstick Liz" about a couple who got in a fight in a bar and she killed her husband. Why that spoke to me might have something to do with my divorce, but that's the one I chose and prayed that it would be okay.

The map to Paul's house was a maze of twists and turns, looking for the cement driveway, pass the oak tree with the reflector, turn left at the white stake, and wind around until I reach the house. The house was a gorgeous old wooden home inside and out nestled between trees and next to Upper Clear Creek.

I arrived early so there was time to get to know who Paul Mitchell was, a pharmaceutical salesman, having spent the last fifteen years covering all of Alaska for Ely Lilly. Now his territory was all of northern California from Sacramento north.

As we walked the property, he shared that his wife of 27 years left him months earlier. Then he pointed out 27 cedar trees he had planted on the property to honor that relationship, yet at this point they were all dead. I thought, well that relationship is definitely over!

Curious about the guests who would be coming, he said they were all doctors and nurses from various offices he visited. Oh dear, how fast can I choose a different poem? After lunch, we all gathered on his large patio by the creek and began to share our poetry. I sat on Paul's right side and was glad he started the reading and directed the next person on his left to share. Just what I was afraid of…the poems were spiritual, loving, caring, bringing out emotions and expressions of appreciation with hands over hearts as one-by-one shared.

My pulse quickened and finally I said to myself, "Okay God, you got me into this, so here goes…" As I started reading, everyone began to look at each other with very questionable looks, wondering what in the hell was going on. But when I was finished, Paul actually yelled, "Robert Service, I love Robert Service poetry!" and everyone laughed. What a relief! It wasn't long before everyone left but me, so we had a wonderful evening getting to know one another.

After a few more evenings together, we came to realize that we were adventurers and spiritual travelers. And a few months later, we realized we were soul mates.

What a gift for both of us. He began taking classes to receive his practitioner license and completed the path to ministry, but his work kept him very busy.

It wasn't long before we moved in together, then bought a house along the Sacramento River. Paul loved to travel and two months after moving in with him, he said, "Let's go to Hawaii!" Shocked, I said I'm from Ohio and we only go to Hawaii after we retire!

He said he's used to going there every year to get a break from the Alaska weather, so how could I refuse! My dream vacation came early. Then he had other ideas for traveling and over the years, we went to San Juan, St. Thomas & Tortola, French Polynesia, Monte Carlo, Florence, Rome, Venice, Naples, Sorrento, Dubrovnik, Istanbul, Barcelona, Rome, Nice, Florence, Amalfi Coast, Netherlands, Germany, Austria, Hungary, Amsterdam, Budapest, Slovakia, Moscow, St. Petersburg, and Thailand.

A train trip from Vancouver BC to Lake Louise. A Maine cruise from Portland to Bar Harbor, Belfast, Rockland, Boothbay Harbor, and Bath. A Columbia River cruise from Clarkston to Astoria to Portland. A Great lakes Cruise from Niagra Falls through all of the Great Lakes with a stop at Mackinac Island, ending up in Detroit, and many other trips on the west coast.

We married after 15 years and enjoyed a total of 33 years together until his passing in November 2024. I miss him greatly. I continue to teach classes and serve as a prayer practitioner and minister at the Center.

I remember the Friday evening right after I retired from the RCD, we were contemplating the next fun adventure to take. The next day, the senior minister of the Center announced she was leaving to lead a church in Washington. Realizing it often takes months to replace a senior minister, Rev. Sue MillerBorn and I offered to be Interim Co-Senior Ministers. It was a great experience. My focus was on the business of the center. Being in the office enabled me to go through every file I could find. I was able to get a $1000 grant and the result was putting together a book, "The History of the Center for Spiritual Living from 1971-2014." It's a great read for those interested in how the Center began and evolved.

F. WRITING FOR FUN

When I moved to California, I joined a group, The Writer's Forum. The first book I published was a series of talks by our Senior Minister, Rev. James Golden. His talks were so powerful for me that I thought it would be great to publish some of them.

And, his motto was "Life is Risky Business." He loved sky diving and took many people from the congregation with him. I hesitated to jump out of a good airplane, so I hired a photographer jump near him and this is a great photo he took.

As the Chips Fall

Based on a true story, Fiber Supply Manager Jennifer Pace buys wood chips from sawmills for Erie Paper Mill. Her new ill-tempered boss, Cal Brasington, alienates his employees and key suppliers with his ethically challenged behavior. Jen's out-of-work husband, Dune, loves their boat, cruising with Ted and friends in the yacht club, and begins an affair with Nikki, a college student. A concerned colleague, Kent, and her dog, Bagley, help Jen build the courage to leave and find her dream job.

Written by Mary Mitchell, 18990 Shoreline Drive, Cottonwood, CA 96022 ©
revmary49@gmail.com (530) 347-0996

Then, I began to write about my experiences in Puget Sound. I tried my hand at writing a movie script, which I titled "As the Chips Fall." I finished it about ten years ago, and it captures much of what is in this memoir. I found an agent in Los Angeles who shared it with many producers. They liked it, but said it didn't have enough sex and violence. Not wanting to add that, especially the thought of anything violent, the script sits in my desk drawer, and the dynamite movie poster I designed hangs on my wall.

G. BOOKS I HAVE PUBLISHED

"Engaging Grace: How to Use the Power of Co-Creation in Daily Life" by Mary E. Schroeder, published by iUniverse, sold through Amazon.com and Summerbreeze Publications. It examines the basic truths of the Universe brought to us through the teachings of great spiritual leaders and how to put these truths into action in our lives.

"The Practitioner Handbook for Spiritual Mind Healing" 1st, 2nd, 3rd, and 4th editions. The first edition included talks by Dr. James Golden. Written by Dr. Mary E. Schroeder/Mitchell, published by iUniverse, sold through Amazon.com and Summerbreeze Publications. This handbook advances one's ability to understand the creative process and the power of our mind, as well as the benefits of immersing oneself in the ongoing process of spiritual enlightenment. By continuing to fine-tune our knowledge of how the Law of the Universe works, our life improves, and we advance in our ability to serve others as licensed practitioners.

"The History of the Center for Spiritual Living, Redding 1971-2014" by Rev. Mary E. Mitchell, published by iUniverse, sold through Amazon.com and Summerbreeze Publications. It is a rich story filled with unique experiences as a small group of spiritual seekers began meeting in someone's living room. When Dr. James and Dr. Andrea Golden led the Center, it flourished. How many ministers take their congregants skydiving? White water rafting? On wilderness treks? Weekends of deep introspection at family retreats in rustic cabins deep in the woods? Working together, dozens of members and friends pounded thousands of nails for an old-fashioned barn raising to build the sanctuary! This is a delightful story about how we all learned to jump into life using the principles for successful living, which became deeply held beliefs that powerfully influenced our lives.

"32 Easy Lessons in Metaphysics and the Science of our Mind" by Mary E. Mitchell, published by Balboa Press. This book reveals the essence of who we are at our most powerful level. When we understand how our mind affects the metaphysical, beyond the physical, it all begins to make sense. There are gold nuggets in this treasure trove to enrich your life's adventure! There is a hidden power that lies beyond the physical, and forces of energy that we can control through the power of our mind. It's true: There is a power for good in the universe, and you can use it.

"My Search for Ancient Wisdom; One Prisoner's Journey of Transformation" by Rev. Dr. Mary E. Mitchell and Dr. Michael Nichols, published by Park Point Press, sold through Amazon.com and Summerbreeze Publications. For over a decade, Rev. Mary facilitated an extraordinary correspondence with Dr. Michael Nichols, who asked for her help in adapting to prison with a sentence of life without parole. This is a book of their letters, which cover Dr. Nichol's transformation from a deadly gangster to what Rev. Mary calls a prison Buddha. The exchanges are substantive, powerful, and revealing.

APPENDIX

1. The number of strikes during this time period heavily impacted the timber and wood products industries in Puget Sound and British Columbia.

1978-79 The longest pulp and paper strike in northwest history was from August 1978 to February 1979. As the strike was soon to end, the New York Times published the following information. During the strike, 15,400 of the union's 22,000 members stopped work at 39 mills owned by 13 companies. They were still out at 31 mills as final negotiations began, while 26 mills were operating to turn out about half the industry's normal production.

1981 Tugboat Strike Slows Commerce Officials with the tugboat owners' group, the Northwest Towboat Association, announced that 1,000 tugboat crewmen began a strike Tuesday afternoon. Wages and fringe benefits are the key issues. Some 25 ships have been idled in Puget Sound ports. The pilots said most of the Seattle and Tacoma berths are too hazardous to risk docking without tugboats, and at least 13 more ships are due to arrive in the next two days, which may face the prospect of waiting weeks or proceeding to other ports.

1981 Canadian sawmills strike from July through November the shutdown of the entire British Columbia forest industry was completed Monday as the 7,300-member Canadian Paper workers Union joined some 45,000 other unionized employees who have been off the job for a week. About 40,000 members of the IWA struck 700 sawmills on July 12 and were joined two days later by the 5,500-member Pulp, Paper, and Woodworkers of Canada.

1986 Weyerhaeuser's 22 sawmills strike from June-Jul Portland, Oregon – Some of the 7,500 workers who went on strike against

Weyerhaeuser Company more than a month ago include the employees who work at 22 Weyerhaeuser mills in Oregon and Washington. About 6,400 members of the IWA will vote next week on a contract offer.

2. **Article in the Port Townsend Leader newspaper by Gina McMather: "Spindly 'Doghair' Timber Becoming Economically Valuable – Forest Service's Quilcene District Discovers New Market for Stale Timber"**

The Leader

A narrow winding path has been hacked into the dense stand of dwarfed trees near Bon Jon Pass. The day is bright and sunny, but little light penetrates the murk under the interlocking boughs. Visibility is virtually zero through the tangle of spindly trunks. It could easily be the setting for a gloomy fairy tale by the Brothers Grimm.

Although the trees are 50 years old, few have attained a diameter of more than several inches. Their growth stopped more than 20 years ago, and an estimated 40,000 trees are crowded onto each acre.

This is a "doghair" stand in the Quilcene District of the Olympic National Forest.

The term 'doghair,' which denotes such overcrowded, stagnated stands, evolved from the expression "thick as the hair on a dog's back." There are about 20,000 acres of dog hair in the Quilcene District, says head Quilcene Ranger Bob Haase. The stands range in density from 2,000 to 40,000 trees per acre with average trunk diameters under eight inches. By comparison, a healthy commercial stand of 80-year-old second-growth timber may average 300-500 trees per acre with diameters of 24-36 inches. What to do about the dog hair is a question that has long plagued the Quilcene District.

"We started worrying about it years and years ago," says Ranger Haase. "We've been studying it for 20-30 years. Soil and fertilization studies were conducted over a ten-year period." The stands were created by fires that occurred between the turn of the century and the 1920s. Reseeding occurred naturally but too well. Fir and western hemlock sprang up profusely, and their growth was checked after a decade or two by the severity of the competition.

The Forest Service studies suggested additional factors contributed to the stagnation. The soil is typically gravelly and low in nutrients, especially nitrogen. The soil beneath the surface is compacted, creating a 'hardpan' barrier difficult for young roots to penetrate. Located in the rain shadow of the Olympic mountains, the stands receive less moisture than those in other areas.

The Forest Service repeatedly sought to answer the following questions: How could the unproductive doghair be turned into marketable timber?

Letting nature take its slow course might not even result in significant improvement, for growth has virtually stopped. Thinning operations yielded disappointing results when the trees were much older than the 15-to-20-year age considered optimum for standard thinning.

The benefit of more sunlight came too late. The trees were incapable of replacing the many lower branches that had died in the upward struggle to find the sun. Neither was fertilization the answer. Thinning and fertilization combined produced some growth, but it was still not enough to make the effort worthwhile.

Quilcene resident and conservationist Tim McNulty has thinned doghair stands for the district and vividly recalls working under the interlocked canopy of branches. "It's like working in a cave. You cut the tree, and it still stands up. You have to wrestle it to the ground."

If the doghair could not grow, the next best hope seemed to be to remove the spindly trees and carefully reforest, a costly alternative. The tiny trees were unmarketable as saw logs. Felling them by conventional methods was prohibitively expensive. In desperation, even burning was considered.

"We started experimenting in 1979," recalls Haase. "With the recession, the lumber market was depressed. As the value of saw logs went down, chips went up." The clean chips required by the paper mills were normally a secondary product of logging operations. With logging slowed down, chips were in short supply. If a way could be found to turn the difficult doghair material into sufficiently clean chips, the conversion might be affordable.

Attempts to log the doghair began in 1980, experimenting with a variety of logging and yarding "removal" techniques. The first efforts were awkward and costly, but gradually, methods and technology were improved. "We started out on a small scale," says Haase. "Now it's on a large scale—kind of like a Saint Bernard puppy."

In 1982, the Forest Service formulated a 20-year plan to rehabilitate the doghair. Funds appropriated to the Forest Service by Congress were funneled into the project. The Quilcene District would pioneer logging and reforestation techniques for converging doghair into productive timber. Transportation and processing techniques developed to achieve total utilization of the felled trees will be applicable to commercial cutting to estimate waste left as slash to be burned.

High on the slopes of Ned Hill overlooking Sequim and the Strait of Juan de Fuca, 300 acres of doghair are being harvested at the rate of 2.55 acres per day. Hermann Brothers of Port Angeles are the loggers operating under a special five-year administrative use contract, which was signed in November of 1983. They had logged Quilcene doghair on several pilot sales and were prepared to make the heavy investment in specialized equipment. For each of the five years, they will harvest 300 acres.

Back in the woods, a mechanical harvester known as a feller-buncher has replaced the usual crew of fellers with power saws. Reminiscent of a grade-B sci-fi monster, the gigantic machine lifts pincered claws. The first arm grasps the trunk of a tree while the 22-inch blades of the second claw shear the trunk at the base. Lifting the severed tree vertically into the air, it deposits the tree to one side. Tree trunks lie stacked in its wake like so many bunches of carrots. At regular intervals, the feller-buncher lops only the top of the tree, leaving a 20-foot trunk to decay naturally. The resulting "snag" is intended to provide a perch and nesting place for resident birds.

When the felling is completed, the yarding crews take over. At one site, a high lead cable system brings bunches of tees slithering down the slope to a loader and the waiting trucks. At another, the "clam bunk skidder" fills its own bay with a truckload of trees and brings them to the landing. With gigantic wheels to minimize ground compaction, it travels forward or backward with equal ease, thus eliminating the necessity of a turnaround. "You don't need rear-view mirrors," chuckles operator Don Love, indicating the windshields both front and back. "You just turn your seat around."

From each of the landings, the truckers maneuver their outsized loads of bristling trees over the network of access roads to the centralized shipping center. "The Forest Service wants to totally utilize the material available on the ground," explains logger Steve Hermann, who conceived of bringing the processing center into the logging area. "In order to accomplish 100% utilization and in order to appropriately supply the markets with the quality of products they demand—clean chips rather than whole-tree dirty chips—it takes a manufacturing area. Transportation of the material in whole-tree form is not possible in a heavy-traffic situation, and it's not economically possible to separate the material from the landings."

The five processing machines of the chipping center serve 300 acres of nearby logging sites. Every four or five months, when the logging operations move to a different area, the processing center follows.

Trees arriving at the processing center are first run through the "delimber" and shorn of their boughs. The "darker" then strips the bark, sending the bare white trunks along the conveyor belt to the clean chipper. Disappearing under a revolving bladed drum, the tree reappears at the far end as a spray of bright wood chips blown into a truck trailer. An average of ten truckloads of clean chips are delivered each day to the paper mill to be rendered into pulp and paper products.

Limbs, tops, and bark are fed into another chipper, which produces "hogged fuel" at the rate of about 8 ½ truckloads per day. The "dirty" hog fuel is used by the mills as a power source.

Across the landing, a conveyor carries logs into the shining circular blade of a portable sawmill. These logs are not doghair but the cedar snags left by the forest fires many years before. The portable sawmill cuts them into 4x4 cants and fencing boards. Edges and trimmings are recycled back through the hogged fuel chipper. Any fir logs of a marketable size are reserved for a local sawmill.

Currently, most of the clean chips and hogged fuel are being delivered to the Port Townsend paper mill. Lesser quantities are sold to Crown Zellerbach and I. T. T. Rayonier in Port Angeles. "The success of the whole depends on each individual operation," says Steve Hermann of the complex system. He is constantly searching for new ways to improve coordination. He hopes timber equipment companies will soon develop delimbing and debarking machines capable of handling more than one tree at a time, which will eliminate frequent bottlenecks.

The steepness of the slopes is another perplexing problem. Of the 20,000 acres of Quilcene District doghair, nearly 12,000 acres are on slopes so steep and loosely graveled that they may never be accessible to heavy equipment. The current development plans have earmarked 7,000 potential acres, much of which exists on slopes over 50% grade, too steep for a feller-buncher. A Spyder walking feller-buncher was tested last summer. While performing as well on steep slopes as on flat terrain, it was not originally designed to do logging work and was subject to frequent breakdowns. Hermann notes that several equipment companies are also working on this problem, and he is hoping that a solution will appear within the year.

Back at the Quilcene Ranger Station, the Forest Service doghair team has other problems to tackle. Begun with two men, the group now consists of four permanent and two seasonal members. Soon, it will grow to nine. The group plans and appraises new units and administers those now being harvested. Members also map road locations and write up environmental assessments.

Plotting which 300 acres to cut each of the five years of the contract is in itself a complicated task. Over 1,000 acres of doghair lie within roadless areas proposed for wilderness status. The Wilderness Bill was recently passed by the US Senate, and the House will resolve this issue if it is signed by the President.

Wildlife considerations exempt other acreage from cutting. Because wildlife in the doghair has not been extensively studied, the doghair team must evaluate the habitat on a site-by-site basis. The common opinion holds that deer and elk prefer a habitat that offers better travel and browsing than the closed doghair stands. Birds and small mammals mainly live in the dog hair.

Forest engineer Bob Wulf, on his road mapping forays, has made significant findings that have affected timber sale layouts. Because the rare Northern Spotted Owls are generally thought to prefer old-growth stands for nesting, he was surprised to encounter some in the dog hair. Three thousand acres were set aside until further study could determine exactly where their nests are. Then, 1,000 acres will be allotted as a study area.

On another trip into the woods, he discovered a blue heron rookery. Bringing several cracked blue eggs and the tiny skeletons of some hapless nestlings back to the station, Wulf turned them over to resource assistant Julie Van Reenan for identification. Not nearly so rare as the owls, the herons were allotted only a few acres necessary to preserve their nests. The rangers joke that they should stop sending Bob Wulf into the forest—they won't have any acreage left.

"We try to control unit sizes to 60 acres," says Doghair Project leader Clark Bainbridge, "although we have the authority to go to

90 acres. We leave strips in between for wildlife and strips along meadows and beaver ponds." He gives Steve Hermann credit for the idea of topping live trees to function as snags for the hawks and cavity-nesting birds.

Conservationist Tim McNulty generally praises the effort to convert the doghair but has reservations about those newly created "snags." "They're trying," he concedes with a sigh, "but it would be nice if some of the old snags were left until the new ones were old enough to provide a habitat. Woodpeckers, bug-eating birds, and hawks, as well as squirrels and chipmunks, depend on them."

Representing Olympic Park Associates and the Washington Wilderness Coalition, McNulty walked areas along Ned Hill with the forest rangers to determine the boundary between the proposed Graywolf Wilderness area and potential logging sites. "We actually did compromise on the wilderness boundary to accommodate some of the sites. It was a reasonable compromise because we couldn't tell the exact watershed divide. We pulled the line a little bit to the south to let them work on the flat." Having worked in the woods a great deal, he feels he has a cordial relationship with the Forest Service.

"They don't see me as a rabid, anti-logging urbanite," he says. However, he does express disappointment over the way the Doghair project was set up. "The conservationists' argument for preserving the roadless is that they generally have poor site capabilities (for logging) but high wildlife and recreational value. The Forest Service should invest time and effort into the lower elevation pre-accessed, more productive lands rather than one-shot cropping of the old growth at higher elevations.

"The doghair project seems to be what the conservationists were looking for. Some of the best (logging) sites are in Doghair. So, the conservationists got behind it so the Forest Service could meet its quotas and take the pressure off the higher sites." The pilot project got into full swing. Then, the Forest Service made it a special project. So now the timber program is going full bore, plus the dog hair. Rather than alleviate the pressure on the marginal high-elevation land, it merely doubles the acreage being cut every year. Be that as it may, they still hope the project is going to be making the land productive." What is seen as a disappointment to conservationists is looked at as good by the Forest Service. "The doghair is specially funded and does not take money from other projects, at least not on our level. The prime areas are all marginal, so there is less of an impact on other loggers or purchasers.

McNulty has no criticism of the logging operation itself, commenting, "They seem to be maximizing existing materials. He believes that road building usually creates more watershed problems than logging operations. Apart from the question of creating new snags for old, he thought the project was making an effort to preserve wildlife and pay attention to the needs of the watershed. He looks forward to seeing the benefits of reforesting. "High priority will be given to closely monitoring the reforestation because that's the goal for the whole process." With a wry face, he adds, "It would be a shame to take out 'umpteen thousands of acres of old doghair only to find they have it replaced it with 'umpteen' thousands of acres of fresh, new doghair."

This is of major concern to the Forest Service as well. Clark Bainbridge checks the new seedlings along the hill on his way to the logging sites. He monitors what planting methods are being used. He is pleased with the seedlings' progress so far. The trees are now two years old and doing fine. They will be thinned at age 15-20 and then fertilized. "If we have noticed when they get to the age of 20 or 30 that the trees stop growing significantly, so we would expect the problems will show up then. We know reducing the competition plus thinning and fertilization will help growth. How much it will help, we don't know."

He observes that white pine seems to do appreciably better under doghair conditions than the fir or hemlock, possibly due to a stronger tap root. In Western forests, the incidence of white pine is usually only about five percent. Its close relative, however, is harvested commercially in the east.

A site near Bon Jon Pass was reforested in white pine. But one by one, the young trees turn bright orange and die, devastated by blister rust. The hardy mature trees that stand unaffected nearby are being studied in hopes of finding a resistant strain. "When we leave snag trees or white pines behind after logging," says Bainbridge, "it's for a purpose." He wished the public was more aware of that fact. "It is illegal to cut such trees for firewood. They serve wildlife and provide natural seeding."

"It is safe to say that the conversion (of doghair) will never pay for itself," says Ranger Haase, discussing the economic aspects of the project. "Of course, if the products' value rises to the point of carrying the program, then it could be put on a profitable basis. But that wouldn't be until the housing or timber market changes, and there appear to be some tough years ahead. The net benefit will still be in our favor. We're talking about a future investment in a renewable resource." The new stand will have been carefully managed, and the roads already be constructed. The investment will be recovered when the seedlings reach maturity and are harvested about the year 2050.

Federal funding recognizes that interim benefits will be derived from the project. The techniques of doghair conversion developed here can be applied elsewhere. Methods of achieving 100 percent utilization of forest materials will be available to the industry as a whole. Federal funds cover 79% of the cost of building permanent roads and maintaining them, plus reforestation, thinning, and fertilization. Road building is normally the most expensive part of a logging operation. The logging company, under its five-year contract, pays a low purchase price and carries the remaining 21% of permanent road building costs and all temporary roads. Some roads were built this past winter, which drove up expenses. Longer-range planning is expected to eliminate the necessity for constructing roads in the off-season.

Steve Hermann declined to give an exact figure for the amount Hermann Brothers have spent on specialized equipment but conceded it was well beyond the million-dollar mark. As efficiency is increased, he hopes the operation will prove profitable for the company. At present, the project supports the employment of 40 persons by Hermann Brothers and nine subcontractors for trucking. The Forest Service doghair staff currently number six, making a total of 55 jobs directly dependent on the project.

Mary Schroeder, Wood Fiber Supply Manager for the Port Townsend Paper Corporation, estimates she buys 50 to 55 truckloads of clean chips (less than 0.5 percent bark) each week from the Hermann Brothers's doghair operation. This represents about ten percent of the mill's total clean chip needs. The doghair-hogged fuel constitutes about 20 percent of the mill's supply. The mill purchases the rest of its chips throughout Puget Sound and British Columbia.

Over the past three years, she has watched chipped products from the dog hair operation improve in quantity and quality. "Everybody said it couldn't be done," she says of the project, because of the difficulty of working in those stands—but they've done it!" The Port Townsend mill provides a key to the marketplace both for clean chips and hogged fuel.

3. Article "Chipping Dog Hair" from the <u>Journal of Logging & Sawmills: Timber West,</u>   Nov/Dec 1982

Lastly, there is an economically feasible harvesting system at work for suppressed 50-80-year-old timber in the Quilcene Ranger District.

Timber here averages less than 8 inches DBH, growing from 2,500 to 40,000 stems per acre on thin, fragile soil—and there are 15,000 acres of this in the area. The timber's quality isn't lacking—it has long fiber, is ideal for high-grade pulp, and has few sizeable logs that produce fine structural lumber. Accessibility isn't a problem either, but its minute size and the ecological necessity of restrictive yarding practices have been stumbling blocks.

Three organizations have a vital interest in the project. The Forest Service wants to manage this ground properly, i.e., harvest the suppressed timber and replant and fertilize the regrowth in order to have a productive forest on these lands. Three logging brothers, Fred, Bill, and Steve Hermann, who are proven innovators, have an idea of a system to do the job economically. And, down at the bottom of the hill—hungry for a continuous supply of wood fiber—is Crown Zellerbach's Port Townsend pulp mill.

District Ranger Bob Haase said they have been searching for over ten years for a way to get the timber going down the road, and they have put up a number of sales in which, unfortunately, the purchasers just couldn't make it no matter what they tried. Hermann Brothers were aware of this situation, and the slow timber economy gave them the time to put their minds to the challenge of this tantalizing situation.

Fortunately, they had appropriate equipment available for the job: a Washington TL-6 for cable yarding, a D-8 for a tail hold cat, a Caterpillar 235 track loader for feeding the Nicholson 22 CTU "Complete Tree Utilizer," and a Cat 227 feller buncher.

Even though the Hermanns had the idea of how to do the job and were willing to carry the financial burden of purchasing the sales and doing the harvesting, they had great respect for the support of the other parties involved. The Hermanns credited the dedication of Mary Schroeder, Crown Zellerbach's Puget Sound Area Fiber Supervisor, and Chuck Goff of the Industrial Forestry Association as instrumental in getting the project accepted by the Forest Service office in Olympia and the regional office in Portland. And Steve Hermann mentioned specifically how much Bob Haase's constant attention has helped the program to run smoothly.

This timber stand is different. Doghair is an apt description. When it was said that there were 40,000 stems to an acre (one per square foot), it was almost unbelievable, but looking at it on the hill, it did seem possible. Steve said, "In some stands, two fellows twenty feet apart can't see one another."

The timber is so badly suppressed there is hardly any perceptible growth in the crowns, and the ring count in the outer third of a cross-section is invisible to the naked eye.

To give us an idea of what had been tried on the site, Haase told of one operator who felled the timber by hand, yarded it with a high-lead machine, and loaded the timber on a log truck. His problem was he couldn't afford to yard, load, and haul the small junk materials.

The Hermanns, by cutting everything on the site down to 10' long and 1" on the butt and bunching all the material in one choker size pile, are getting all possible chip material to the roadside economically.

The System – Two feller bunchers were at work—one a new Cat 227 and the other a Finning Tractor Co. modified Cat 225.

245

The ground on the units we saw was favorable for feller bunchers—even slopes varying from level to 25% grades. These machines are capable of climbing a 40% slope and working efficiently in this attitude.

The timber is bunched butt first in line with the direction of yarding. The multitude of Christmas-size trees handled is unbelievable. Bill Hermann's reply to our amazement was, "Heck, in some places, we have to cut old-growth rhododendrons."

Yarding distance is limited to six hundred feet. A tractor traverses' boundaries, serving as a tail-hold for the haul-back blocks. The stems are just too small for this purpose.

Finding adequate stumps for the one guyline on the Washington TL-6 cable yarder is a problem at times. Fortunately, this machine is very stable and can be carried by one guyline.

The Nicholson 22 CTU chipper fits this work well, according to Bill Hermann. Its drum-style chipper and wide infeed conveyor handle trees with limbs and brush especially well. There is no lost time getting the bushy stems centered; the V drum does this automatically. Because it is an in-line machine and unloads chips right off the back of the machine, as compared with other machines that unload off to one side and have to be parked at an angle on the road, they can get by with a narrower road.

Bill interjected at this point that they are responsible for designing and building the roads—including rocking. A wider road would cost more money.

And he added, "We bid the shows on a lump sum per acre basis." They feel the Forest Service benefits from working with them in this manner because the Forest Service doesn't have to enlarge their staff to do the planning and engineering until they have a grasp of what is involved. But the Hermanns are looking forward to the day when criteria for this system are established, and they can chuck the site layout and road building responsibilities.

Bill was outspoken about the good attitude of their crew toward the different and difficult working conditions of this job, pointing to the rigging crew, as one example, picking up small stems that had fallen off previously yarded turns and throwing them onto the next bundle. He also spoke of the tedium the feller buncher operators were experiencing when cutting all the small twigs.

The precision of their moves is another example of why they are doing well. There is only five to ten minutes lost production time for a 150 to 200-foot move.

A chip truck that has dropped its van backs into the 5th wheel attachment of the chipper, and by the time this unit is moving, the TL-6 yarder has moved and is yarding in the first bundle, which the Cat 235 loader will have ready for the chipper when it is in place.

To produce 10 to 12 van loads per day, working with the class of material that they are and moving 3-4 times a day, is remarkable.

The following is my simple brochure on negotiation. It is printed in landscape and folded in the middle. You'll get the idea.

3. The Plain Vanilla Approach to Negotiation

By Dr. Mary E. Mitchell

Who achieves their goal?

Do you really know the marketplace? Why do people do what they do?

How do you handle power plays and hidden agendas?

Have you identified all the pieces of the puzzle?

Summerbreeze Publications

© 2010

My Experience in the Puget Sound Wood Basket

During the 1980s, I spent years negotiating contracts in the Puget Sound timber, wood products, and pulp and paper industries. The marketplace was so volatile, it required quarterly price and sometimes quantity negotiations with dozens of suppliers and barge, rail, and trucking companies.

One of my assistant buyers was frustrated with the tough and arrogant personalities we dealt with and baffled about why people do what they do. I reflected on how I learned the art of negotiation, which seemed pretty simple at the time.

A few components of the business:

Logs are often rafted to a sawmill or delivered by trucks. The logs are cut into various sizes of lumber or used for other wood products like plywood. Wood waste from the sawmill includes chips and sawdust, transported by barge, truck or rail and is used to make pulp and paper. Bark is burned at both facilities to create electricity.

Bales of pulp and rolls of paper ready for sale.

The Techniques I Learned

In trying to help my employee, I took a detailed look at how I approached every negotiation. After I put this list together, the only way I could describe it was: It's like vanilla ice cream, plain and simple, nothing fancy. The good news is my employee caught on quickly and became a successful negotiator.

My ten tips for a successful negotiation are:

1. Know your market intimately. What is going on in every aspect of the marketplace that even slightly impacts the product or the volume of products you are negotiating on? Hours spent in research are as valuable as gold.

2. Recognize that people are doing what's in their own best interest, which is not usually in your best interest.

3. Always be reliable and consistent. If the other person is not, this is to your advantage, because they're not likely to be as thoroughly prepared as you.

4. Out of respect, always be on time for a negotiation. If the other person is not, it's likely a power play, and don't let it bother you. Let them know their being late was perfect, because you had other more important things to take care of.

5. Another power play is to sit you in a corner or on a chair that puts you lower than their eye level. Ignore it and relax. It's likely they're not as prepared as you, since they expected this simple imbalance of power would give them leverage.

6. When meeting in the other person's space, scan the environment in detail. Observe papers, books, photos on the wall, notes on the desk, everything. It's fascinating what you'll learn about who this person is and what they're trying to tell you about themself. Don't ask about any of it, just take it in.

7. You may walk into their office filled with things that reflect their ego. They expect you to be impressed and admire their wall of awards, animal heads, pictures of a fish they caught, etc. They expect that you'll think they're better at something than you are. Ignore it and get down to business. It immediately changes the energy in the room and levels the balance of power.

8. They likely assume their ego display will stimulate you to find some common ground for negotiation. Don't take the bait. Don't ask things like, "So where is this amazing fishing hole?" It's a ploy to soften you up so that when pressed, you won't negotiate in your best interest. In reality, they're so self-focused, they aren't as prepared as you.

9. The importance of ignoring any ego display is that it throws them off balance. They initially expect to talk about themselves for ten minutes before getting down to business. They're trying to show you how really cool they are, so don't take the bait. Let their mind stay busy, wondering why you aren't impressed. Stick to business and you'll succeed, because you're thoroughly prepared and you take this

business seriously. Negotiating with someone surrounded by their ego display is easy!

10. Use the same principle in reverse. If you invite someone to your office for a negotiation, don't have any ego items on the wall. Clear your desk. Be totally focused on the negotiation. I've watched many negotiators waste time trying to soften each other up or find common interests that would result in a deal that makes both parties happy, but that is not what you were hired to do.

When you're not prepared, it's easy to get tripped up, and they will be delighted to remember that as your weak spot. Whatever the negotiation is about, be prepared. Negotiations are delightfully fun when the market price is fluid and sometimes volatile.

In Conclusion

Negotiating is like a puzzle. Identify all of the pieces that put up or down pressure on the price or quantity of a product. Create a checklist with room to note the degree of up or down pressure it puts on the price or volume.

CHECKLIST

The answer of whether to go for a price increase or decrease will be obvious and, in my experience, it just 'falls out of the bottom.'

Enjoy the hunt!

www.ingramcontent.com/pod-product-compliance
Lightning Source LLC
Chambersburg PA
CBHW051302120626
46547CB00015B/2047